ROCK 'n' ROLL
CHRONICLES
1955-1963

ROCK'n'ROLL
CHRONICLES
1955-1963

Longmeadow Press

Photographic Acknowledgments
BMI/Michael Ochs Archives – Venice, CA: 49 left, 71 right, 94 left.
Camera Press: 2 main, 4/5, 7 inset, 49 right, 50 main.
Harry Hammond/London Features International: 57.
Richie Howell/Redferns: 2 inset, 3, 6, 22, 39, 66.
London Features International: 8, 15 right, 47, 55 main, 67, 75, 101, 103, 109 left, 114, 123.
Michael Ochs Archives – Venice, CA: 9, 10 left and right, 11, 12, 13, 16, 17, 18 inset, 19, 20, 23, 24 left and right, 26 left and right, 27, 28 left, 29, 30, 31 right, 32 right, 33, 35 left and right, 40 top and bottom, 41, 42, 43, 44, 46, 48, 50 inset, 51 left and right, 52 left and right, 54, 55 inset, 58, 59, 61 left and right, 62 left and right, 63, 64, 65, 68, 70 left and right, 71 left, 73, 77, 79, 81 main and inset, 84, 85 left and right, 88, 90 left, 91, 92, 93 main and inset, 94 right, 95, 96, 98, 100, 102 left and right, 104, 108, 109 right, 110, 111, 113 left and right, 115 left, 116, 117, 118, 119 right, 121, 122 right, 124.
Michael Ochs Archives/London Features International: 18, 36, 38, 72, 90 right, 119 left.
David Redfern/Redferns: 37, 69 top and bottom, 82, 83, 86, 97, 99, 105, 112, 120.
Rex Features: 15 left, 21, 28 right, 34, 53, 76, 89, 107.
Robert Hunt Library: 32 left, 45, 60, 115 right.
Robert Smith/Redferns: 7 main.
C Stewart/Redferns: 74

The photographs on pages 14, 25, 56, 78, 80, 87 and 106 by Harry Hammond are taken from *Hit Parade* by Harry Hammond and Gered Mankowitz, published by Plexus Publishing. Those on pages 31 (left) and 122 (left), are from *The Rock Lists Album* by Plexus Publishing.

Cover Photographs

Front cover
Main picture: Elvis Presley (Robert Hunt Library)
Inset left: The Beatles (Camera Press)
Inset top right: Connie Francis (Cyrus Andrews/Redferns)
Inset centre right: Everly Brothers (David Redfern/Redferns)
Inset bottom right: Ray Charles (David Redfern/Redferns)

Back cover
Main picture: (Robert Smith/Redferns)
Inset top: Little Stevie Wonder (David Redfern/Redferns)
Inset centre: Buddy Holly (Rex Features)
Inset bottom: Brenda Lee (Hulton-Deutsch)

This 1991 edition is published by
Longmeadow Press
201 High Ridge Road
Stamford, Connecticut 06904

Copyright © 1991
Brian Trodd Publishing House Limited

American chart information is
© 1991 BPI Communications, Inc.
Used with permission from *Billboard*

ISBN 0-681-41178-3

Printed in Italy

Contents

Introduction

The *Rock'n'Roll Chronicles* will chart the history of that music variously known as rock'n'roll, pop and just plain rock. In this volume, it's the story of rock'n'roll we're concerned with, from the coming of Elvis through to the Beatles. These were the formative years of a whole new musical genre, bursting at the seams with revolutionary sounds. Much of the music sounds every bit as fresh and challenging today, flowing out of sophisticated sound systems, as it did then, struggling to escape the confines of a diner jukebox or Dansette record-player.

The story is told month by month, with the key records and events highlighted, their significance explored. The top tens are the *first* from each calendar month. The illustrations, as much as is possible, correspond to the dates in the text.

Of course it's not possible to keep one's own tastes and prejudices out of a book like this, but we've done our best (most of the time, anyway). The evolution of rock over the last four decades is a fascinating and important subject. We hope we've done it justice.

STEVE MONNERY and GARY HERMAN

1955

1955 was not so much the year rock'n'roll was born as the year in which the infant music took its first unsupported steps. Bill Haley's 'Rock around the Clock' hit #1 in the US, Elvis Presley's fame began to spread like a fast-moving storm, and black artists like Chuck Berry, Little Richard and Bo Diddley suddenly found a music and a white teenage audience that went together.

After three decades of familiarity it's hard to appreciate just how astonishing the new music and musicians sounded and looked to audiences raised in the austere and repressive atmosphere of the post-war decade. This was music that took risks, that challenged and threatened not only the musical conventions of the age, but conventional notions of the way people lived, most notably in attitudes towards sex and race.

Such a wild child would eventually be tamed, domesticated, made safe, but for these few months it roamed wild and free, infecting a generation with the excitement of a music that moved.

Little Richard

American popular music, in the early '50s, is a matter of musics. There's pop itself, mostly ballads and singalongs with an occasional novelty thrown in, there's Country and Western, and there's Rhythm and Blues (R&B). These are more than mere musical styles – they are musics made for and by specific social groups. The country audience is predominantly rural, white and confined to the American South and West. Rhythm and blues is for blacks. Pop is for the rest.

The story of the mid-'50s is largely the story of boundaries blurring, of different musics cross-fertilizing to meet the demands of a new teenage audience.

As 1955 begins, the process is already well underway. R&B, itself a post-war synthesis of blues and big band music, is the fastest growing sector of the record business, thanks to hugely increased sales to white teenagers. Disc jockeys like Alan Freed (who calls the music 'rock'n'roll' to avoid the racial connotations of 'rhythm and blues') have been promoting it for several years, on the air and in concerts. The most popular black artists – like Fats Domino, the Drifters, the Moonglows – are no longer heard only in the ghetto.

The music trickles down through American society, inspiring white artists to infuse old country and pop forms with black music's rhythmic excitement. Bill Haley and the Comets have already had minor hits with beat-laden dance band records, and in Memphis Sun Records' owner Sam Phillips has signed up one poor southern white boy who sings country or blues with rhythm to spare – Elvis Presley.

'Hail, hail, rock'n'roll' – Alan
Freed on the air

USA

1 **Mr Sandman**
Chordettes

2 **Let Me Go, Lover**
Joan Weber

3 **Naughty Lady Of Shady Lane**
Ames Brothers

4 **This Ole House**
Rosemary Clooney

5 **Count Your Blessings**
Eddie Fisher

6 **I Need You Now**
Eddie Fisher

7 **Teach Me Tonight**
De Castro Sisters

8 **Hearts of Stone**
Fontane Sisters

9 **Papa Loves Mambo**
Perry Como

10 **Let Me Go, Lover**
Teresa Brewer

UK

1 **Mambo Italiano**
Rosemary Clooney

2 **Finger of Suspicion**
Dickie Valentine

3 **Mr Sandman**
The Chordettes

4 **Shake Rattle and Roll**
Bill Haley

5 **Naughty Lady of Shady Lane**
Dean Martin

6 **Happy Days and Lonely Nights**
Suzi Miller

7 **No One But You**
Billy Eckstine

8 **Softly Softly**
Ruby Murray

9 **Don't Go to Strangers**
Ronnie Harris

10 **Let Me Go**
Teresa Brewer

For the first time 45s outsell 78s, but in some people's minds it's the wrong ones that are being bought. LaVern Baker's original recording of 'Tweedle Dee' has been overtaken on the national charts by Georgia Gibbs' cover version – Baker being black, Gibbs white. This is not an unusual occurrence, but – a sign of the times – Baker decides to do something about it, and appeals to Congress to revise the law so as to prevent such note-for-note copying practices.

Nothing much is done, and the practice will linger on into the 60s. In the meantime good taste will prove more effective than the legal process: more and more DJs are giving greater airplay to the originals, which gives audiences the chance to hear how much better they usually are than the copies.

Bucking this trend, on the 19th Dot Records announce the signing of their new singing sensation, one Pat Boone. A crooner at heart, Boone soon learns that a large part of his new job is copying black R&B records, which he does with great commercial success for several years. In the process he offers living proof that making rock'n'roll respectable and emasculating it are two facets of the same process.

Johnny Ace is already dead, but he's still more in tune with the age to come than Pat Boone. 'Pledging My Love' reaches #1 on the R&B chart two months after the singer has shot himself dead playing Russian Roulette, setting a style for rock'n'roll casualties that will endure at least as long as his music.

EP sleeve 50's style. Inset: Pat Boone checking out his identity

USA

1 **Let Me Go, Lover**
Joan Weber

2 **Mr Sandman**
Chordettes

3 **Hearts of Stone**
Fontane Sisters

4 **Naughty Lady of Shady Lane**
Ames Brothers

5 **Sincerely**
McGuire Sisters

6 **Melody of Love**
Billy Vaughn

7 **That's All I Want From You**
Jaye P. Morgan

8 **No More**
Dejohn Sisters

9 **Make Yourself Comfortable**
Sarah Vaughan

10 **Teach Me Tonight**
De Castro Sisters

UK

1 **Mambo Italiano**
Rosemary Clooney

2 **Finger of Suspicion**
Dickie Valentine

3 **Softly Softly**
Ruby Murray

4 **Shake Rattle and Roll**
Billy Haley

5 **Naughty Lady of Shady Lane**
Dean Martin

6 **Give Me Your Word**
Tennessee Ernie Ford

7 **Let Me Go**
Teresa Brewer

8 **Mobile**
Ray Burns

9 **A Blossom Fell**
Various Artists

10 **Mr Sandman**
The Chordettes

USA

1 **Sincerely**
McGuire Sisters

2 **Hearts of Stone**
Fontane Sisters

3 **Melody of Love**
Billy Vaughn

4 **Ko Ko Mo**
Perry Como

5 **Tweedle Dee**
Georgia Gibbs

6 **Crazy Otto Medley**
Johnny Maddox

7 **That's All I Want From You**
Jaye P. Morgan

8 **Earth Angel**
Crew Cuts

9 **Earth Angel**
Penguins

10 **Ko Ko Mo**
Crew Cuts

UK

1 **Give Me Your Word**
Tennessee Ernie Ford

2 **Softly Softly**
Ruby Murray

3 **Let Me Go**
Teresa Brewer

4 **Naughty Lady of Shady Lane**
Dean Martin

5 **Shake Rattle and Roll**
Bill Haley

6 **Mambo Italiano**
Rosemary Clooney

7 **Mobile**
Ray Burns

8 **Heartbeat**
Ruby Murray

9 **Finger of Suspicion**
Dickie Valentine

10 **A Blossom Fell**
Nat 'King' Cole

On the 10th Atlantic bosses Ahmet Ertegun and Jerry Wexler present Ruth Brown with a special gold record in recognition of the 5 million records she's sold over the last six years. In the previous year she's had two number ones on the R&B chart, but they'll be her last. Though Brown will carry on selling prolifically throughout the decade in the R&B market, her crossover success in the pop charts will be minimal.

On the other side of the Atlantic, and of music, Irish female crooner Ruby Murray has her fourth and fifth Top Ten UK entries. Teresa Brewer, Dickie Valentine, Rosemary Clooney and Dean Martin all have records in the British Top Ten. It will require several years, and the development of a new pop mainstream out of rock'n'roll, before this old mainstream can be relegated to the easy listening racks.

Generally speaking, the US charts are dominated by white pop covers of R&B hits like the Crew-Cuts' 'Earth Angel' and the McGuire Sisters' 'Sincerely' (copied from, respectively, the Penguins' and the Moonglows' originals). One exception, which hits #1 as the month ends, is Bill Hayes' 'Ballad of Davy Crockett'. There will be eight other versions of this song, all of them by white artists. The market in fur hats is booming.

Another song destined to spawn a thousand versions – 'Unchained Melody' from the film *Unchained* – is released in three of them. Roy Hamilton will make #6, Al Hibbler #3, Les Baxter the top spot. The latter two will also do well in Britain, despite competition from future housewives' DJ Jimmy Young.

Some music comes but once. In New York, on the 12th, jazz saxophonist Charlie 'Bird' Parker dies of heart failure at the age of 34.

50's R & B star Ruth Brown

On the 1st Elvis Presley's fourth single is released by Sun. Like the others it has a country-based song on one side, a blues-based song on the other. The latter, 'Baby, Let's Play House', is his first release to feature drums, but that's not the only reason it's astonishing. Rock writer Greil Marcus will later muse that 'for pure excitement, he may never have matched it', and the sense of liberated energy, of triumph in his own talent, pours from the performance like a dream coming true.

A talent like this takes some getting used to. Later in the month Elvis goes to New York for a show audition, and loses out to Pat Boone.

'Davy Crockett' still tops the charts in the US; in the UK, Tennessee Ernie Ford's 'Give Me Your Word' is nearing the end of a seven-week run at #1. Ford has had several years' success with his style of country-verging-on-Middle-of-the-Road, but after hitting gold later in the year with the novelty 'Sixteen Tons' he will beat the traditional path into mainstream showbiz.

Johnnie Ray is touring the UK, and enjoying his first chart success there with 'If You Believe'. Though apparently white he has Blackfoot ancestors, and has a most un-Waspish line in emotional histrionics. His success in the R&B market has been an important factor in the breaking down of American musical frontiers.

USA

1 **The Ballad of Davy Crockett**
Billy Hayes

2 **Crazy Otto Medley**
Johnny Maddox

3 **Sincerely**
McGuire Sisters

4 **Tweedle Dee**
Georgia Gibbs

5 **Melody of Love**
Billy Vaughn

6 **Ko Ko Mo**
Perry Como

7 **Ballad of Davy Crockett**
Fess Parker

8 **How Important Can It Be**
Joni James

9 **Open Up Your Heart**
Cowboy Church
Sunday School

10 **Earth Angel**
Crew Cuts

UK

1 **Give Me Your Word**
Tennessee Ernie Ford

2 **Softly Softly**
Ruby Murray

3 **Cherry Pink and Apple Blossom White**
Perez Prado

4 **A Blossom Fell**
Nat 'King' Cole

5 **Prize of Gold**
Joan Regan

6 **Mobile**
Ray Burns

7 **If Anyone Finds This I Love You**
Ruby Murray

8 **Tomorrow**
Johnny Brandon

9 **Mambo Rock**
Bill Haley

10 **Let Me Go**
Teresa Brewer

Johnnie Ray – angst to spare

Rock'n'roll may win the war, but in the meantime there are battles to be fought. On the 13th Elvis Presley's performance at a Jacksonville concert is good enough to start a riot. He escapes uninjured, but minus most of his clothes.

Four days later, a student at Princeton starts blaring 'Rock around the Clock' out of his window. Others follow suit, and still more wander round the campus singing the song at the tops of their voices. But then the Dean wakes up, tells them to shut up, and they do.

These, of course, are responsible students. If the general public is exposed to this music who knows what may happen? On the 22nd a Fats Domino concert in Bridgeport is cancelled by the police, just in case a real riot does take place.

As if to add substance to such fears, Bo Diddley's first single, named after himself, appears on the R&B charts. 'Bo Diddley' is black, rhythmic and menacing – in fact all the things white America has been warning its children against.

Another, even more auspicious, debut is in the offing. After playing guitar in a St Louis trio for three years, Chuck Berry has been pushed in the direction of Chess Records by Muddy Waters, and on the 21st he goes into their Chicago studio to record the self-penned 'Maybellene'.

The guitar is mixed further back and the style more blues-based than will later be the case, but the heavy backbeat and playful lyrics are archetypal Chuck Berry. 'Maybellene' is one of the first head-on collisions between rockabilly and the city.

Chuck 'Beret'

USA

1 **Cherry Pink and Apple Blossom White**
Perez Prado

2 **Ballad of Davy Crockett**
Billy Hayes

3 **Dance With Me, Henry**
Georgia Gibbs

4 **Crazy Otto Medley**
Johnny Maddox

5 **Unchained Melody**
Les Baxter

6 **Ballad of Davy Crockett**
Tennessee Ernie Ford

7 **Ballad of Davy Crockett**
Fess Parker

8 **Unchained Melody**
Al Hibbler

9 **Tweedle Dee**
Georgia Gibbs

10 **Darling Je Vous Aime Beaucoup**
Nat 'King' Cole

UK

1 **Stranger in Paradise**
Tony Bennett

2 **Cherry Pink and Apple Blossom White**
Perez Prado

3 **Earth Angel**
The Crew Cuts

4 **Cherry Pink and Apple Blossom White**
Eddie Calvert

5 **Give Me Your Hand**
Tennessee Ernie Ford

6 **Stranger in Paradise**
Tony Martin

7 **Ready Willing and Able**
Doris Day

8 **Wedding Bells**
Eddie Fisher

9 **If You Believe**
Johnnie Ray

10 **You, My Love**
Frank Sinatra

Teenage rebellion movies are not new, but whereas Marlon Brando's *The Wild One* and James Dean's *Rebel without a Cause* have conventional musical scoring, the newly released *Blackboard Jungle* has rock'n'roll. In one famous scene the connection is dramatized. A hapless teacher, trying to interest his students in music, plays them records from his treasured jazz collection. They're not interested – it's not *their* music – and end up throwing his records round the classroom. Music has become a measure of the distance between generations.

The music the students want, the music that plays over the opening credits, is Bill Haley and the Comets' 'Rock around the Clock', and as the film shows across America the record, released the previous year as a 'B' side, inexorably advances up the charts. It will hit #1 in early July and stay there for eight weeks.

Haley's music represents only a slight shift, but it's enough to tip the balance. Though the vocals and instrumentation are those of the traditional small white dance band, the rhythm is R&B and, most crucially, utterly predominant.

A year earlier Pat Boone and Fats Domino would have climbed their respective charts (pop and R&B) with 'Ain't That a Shame', but now Domino is also climbing the pop chart. True, he'll only reach #10 to Boone's #1, but the 'music's' on the wall.

Two future giants of country are putting down markers. Johnny Cash's first Sun single is released a month after the birth of his daughter (and future star) Rosanne, and in Nashville Patsy Cline makes her Grand Ole Opry debut.

USA

1 **Cherry Pink and Apple Blossom White**
Perez Prado

2 **Unchained Melody**
Les Baxter

3 **Dance with Me, Henry**
Georgia Gibbs

4 **Ballad of Davy Crockett**
Billy Hayes

5 **Unchained Melody**
Al Hibbler

6 **Ballad of Davy Crockett**
Fess Parker

7 **Ballad of Davy Crockett**
Tennessee Ernie Ford

8 **A Blossom Fell**
Nat 'King' Cole

9 **Unchained Melody**
Roy Hamilton

10 **Rock around the Clock**
Bill Haley

UK

1 **Stranger in Paradise**
Tony Bennett

2 **Unchained Melody**
Al Hibbler

3 **Cherry Pink and Apple Blossom White**
Perez Prado

4 **Cherry Pink**
Eddie Calvert

5 **Earth Angel**
The Crew Cuts

6 **If You Believe**
Johnnie Ray

7 **Give Me Your Hand**
Tennessee Ernie Ford

8 **Unchained Melody**
Jimmy Young

9 **Stranger in Paradise**
The Four Aces

10 **Stranger in Paradise**
Tony Martin

Bill Haley and the Comets – go, daddio, go!

The King of Western Bop and (inset) his first single release

Elvis's 'Baby, Let's Play House' is his first national chart entry, reaching #10 on the Billboard country listing. He buys his first Cadillac, hopefully remembering the lines of the song that's paying for it – 'You may have a pink Cadillac, but doncha be nobody's fool!' In the Memphis studios he cuts what will prove his last recordings for Sun: 'I Forgot to Remember to Forget', 'Tryin' to Get to You' and 'Tomorrow Night'.

Meanwhile entrepreneur Colonel Tom Parker, who wants to be Elvis's manager (and will be, once Bob Neal's contract expires in November), is spreading the word beyond the South through his contacts in radio and music publishing.

Suddenly the 'King of Western Bop' is filling the airwaves of New York and Cleveland.

No such joys afflict Britain's teenagers. Alma Cogan's 'Dreamboat' starts the month at #1; it will be toppled by Slim Whitman's 'Rose Marie', which will go on to spend a record 11 weeks at the top. The rest of the chart is full of unchained melodies, Dickie Valentine, Rosemary Clooney, Tony Bennett and Frankie Laine. Ballads one and all, ranging from the lilting to the melodramatic. In this context 'Earth Angel', albeit the sanitized Crew-Cuts version, seems almost futuristic. Rock'n'roll is yet to arrive on this side of the Atlantic.

One new release of interest in the US is Les Paul and Mary Ford's 'Hummingbird'. It will be the last Top Ten hit for the guitarist and singer, reaching #7, and in the long run Les Paul will be remembered more for creating the electric guitar which bears his name and for inventing the first eight-track recorder.

USA

1 **Cherry Pink and Apple Blossom White**
Perez Prado

2 **Unchained Melody**
Les Baxter

3 **Rock around the Clock**
Bill Haley

4 **A Blossom Fell**
Nat 'King' Cole

5 **Learnin' the Blues**
Frank Sinatra

6 **Honey Babe**
Art Mooney

7 **Dance with Me, Henry**
Georgia Gibbs

8 **Unchained Melody**
Al Hibbler

9 **Something's Gotta Give**
McGuire Sisters

10 **Something's Gotta Give/Love Me or Leave Me**
Sammy Davis, jnr.

UK

1 **Unchained Melody**
Al Hibbler

2 **Dreamboat**
Alma Cogan

3 **Unchained Melody**
Jimmy Young

4 **Earth Angel**
The Crew Cuts

5 **Cherry Pink and Apple Blossom White**
Eddie Calvert

6 **Stranger in Paradise**
Tony Bennett

7 **I Wonder**
Dickie Valentine

8 **Cool Water**
Frankie Laine

9 **Cherry Pink and Apple Blossom White**
Perez Prado

10 **Where Will the Dimple Be**
Rosemary Clooney

The campaign against copy covers advances on several fronts. On the 13th one record company, Savoy, demands that anyone wishing to make a cover version gets permission from the copyright office. The following week the New York radio station WINS announces a new policy: it will not play covers that slavishly copy either the instrumental arrangement or vocal phrasing of other recordings. Specifically banished from their playlist are Pat Boone's 'Ain't That a Shame', Georgia Gibbs' 'Tweedle Dee' and Johnny Long's 'Maybellene'. The last-named has, in any case, significantly failed to take any sales away from Chuck Berry's fast-climbing original.

Bill Haley's records have arrived in London, and are being used as threatening weapons. After telling his neighbours he'll drive them mad, one Londoner plays 'Shake, Rattle and Roll' at mega-volume for most of a sunny afternoon. The judge fines him three pounds ten shillings for 'creating an abominable noise'.

Sun releases the fifth Elvis Presley single – 'Mystery Train'/'I Forgot to Remember to Forget' – amid mounting speculation (much of it apparently fuelled by Colonel Parker) as to which of the big companies will eventually prise him away. Chuck Berry's 'Maybellene' takes over from Fats Domino's 'Ain't That a Shame' as the R&B #1 for a nine-week run.

On the 20th Bo Diddley plays the Apollo in Harlem, fronting the band that will support him for ten years, including his half-sister.

Bo Diddley (left) with maraca-wielding friend

USA

1 **Rock around the Clock**
Bill Haley

2 **A Blossom Fell**
Nat 'King' Cole

3 **Learnin' the Blues**
Frank Sinatra

4 **Cherry Pink and Apple Blossom White**
Perez Prado

5 **Ain't That a Shame**
Pat Boone

6 **Hard to Get**
Giselle Mackenzie

7 **Unchained Melody**
Les Baxter

8 **Something's Gotta Give**
McGuire Sisters

9 **It's a Sin to Tell a Lie**
S. Smith & The Redheads

10 **Something's Gotta Give**
Sammy Davis, jnr.

UK

1 **Rose Marie**
Slim Whitman

2 **Cool Water**
Frankie Laine

3 **Unchained Melody**
Jimmy Young

4 **Strange Lady in Town**
Frankie Laine

5 **Ev'ry Day of My Life**
Malcolm Vaughan

6 **Evermore**
Ruby Murray

7 **Ev'rywhere**
David Whitfield

8 **Dreamboat**
Alma Cogan

9 **Learnin' the Blues**
Frank Sinatra

10 **I Wonder**
Dickie Valentine

The Platters' first million-seller, 'Only You', enters the pop charts. The group has only been signed by Mercury as a makeshift in a deal involving the Penguins, but the Platters will prove to be the biggest-selling black group of the 50's, with four number ones over the next three years.

On the 30th James Dean dies in a car smash. In only three films he has created a personal image of heartfelt, inarticulate and youthful rebellion which will now never need to be compromised. Two weeks earlier, in a New Orleans studio, one of rock'n'roll's formative figures has made his recording debut for Specialty, and in the process turned inarticulacy into a statement of breathtaking clarity.

Little Richard, after trying out several songs that are less than earth-shattering, starts fooling around during a break with a scurrilous little ditty called 'Tutti Frutti'. Someone says they like the sound, and once someone else (Dorothy La Bosterie) has been found to clean up the lyrics the song is recorded, and the record launched onto a largely unsuspecting world.

'Tutti Frutti' is a frontal assault, strengthened rather than weakened by the idiocy of its lyrics. There is no attempt to communicate with anything other than the sound, and the sound itself – berserk vocal, blaring rhythm, caterwauling sax – makes no concessions. Both on record and on stage, in his refusal to recognize any conventional notion of restraint, Little Richard tosses, with joyous contempt, a gauntlet at America's feet.

USA

1 **Rock around the Clock**
Bill Haley
2 **Ain't That a Shame**
Pat Boone
3 **Yellow Rose of Texas**
Mitch Miller
4 **Learnin' the Blues**
Frank Sinatra
5 **Hard to Get**
Giselle Mackenzie
6 **Yellow Rose of Texas**
Johnny Desmond
7 **Seventeen**
Boyd Bennett
8 **A Blossom Fell**
Nat 'King' Cole
9 **House of Blue Lights**
Chuck Miller
10 **Maybellene**
Chuck Berry

UK

1 **Rose Marie**
Slim Whitman
2 **Cool Water**
Frankie Laine
3 **Learnin' the Blues**
Frank Sinatra
4 **Ev'rywhere**
David Whitfield
5 **The Breeze and I**
Caterina Valente
6 **Indian Love Call**
Slim Whitman
7 **Strange Lady in Town**
Frankie Laine
8 **Ev'ry Day of My Life**
Malcolm Vaughan
9 **Evermore**
Ruby Murray
10 **John and Julie**
Eddie Calvert

The man who broke the mould –
Little Richard

October 1955

ubbock, Texas, plays host to Bill Haley and Elvis Presley on consecutive nights in mid-month, and both shows are opened by a local rockabilly duo. Buddy (Holly) and Bob (Montgomery) have been popular in the area for a couple of years, with a regular radio spot and several recorded demos to their name. Their music is country-based, but like everyone else they've been influenced by the year's changes, and the rockabilly element is now growing stronger.

In the Haley audience one agent sees the potential in Holly, and seeks to arrange a recording session for him with Decca in Nashville. Holly is loth to abandon Montgomery, but the latter, with a generosity which will later find reward in a writing, publishing and production career, insists his friend takes the offered chance.

One auspicious new release is the Robins' 'Smokey Joe's Cafe'. The song unfolds a vignette of urban reality, complete with characters and atmosphere, in three minutes of music. It is written, and the record produced, by Jerry Leiber and Mike Stoller. Over the last few years the twosome have built a reputation in both fields which future work with Elvis Presley, the Coasters and the Drifters will further enhance.

In the UK *Blackboard Jungle* is finally released and, as in the US, 'Rock around the Clock' begins a parallel climb up the charts. It's the record's second entry, but whereas the first peaked at #17, this one will go all the way.

Chuck Berry. Inset: Jerry Lieber and Mike Stoller

USA

1 **Yellow Rose of Texas**
Mitch Miller

2 **Love is a Many-Splendored Thing**
Four Aces

3 **Autumn Leaves**
Roger Williams

4 **Ain't That a Shame**
Pat Boone

5 **Moments to Remember**
Four Lads

6 **Yellow Rose of Texas**
Johnny Desmond

7 **Tina Marie**
Perry Como

8 **Rock around the Clock**
Bill Haley

9 **Maybellene**
Chuck Berry

9 **Seventeen**
Fontane Sisters

UK

1 **Cool Water**
Frankie Laine

2 **Rose Marie**
Slim Whitman

3 **The Man from Laramie**
Jimmy Young

4 **Learnin' the Blues**
Frank Sinatra

5 **Ev'rywhere**
David Whitfield

6 **Indian Love Call**
Slim Whitman

7 **The Breeze and I**
Caterina Valente

8 **Blue Star**
Cyril Stapleton

9 **Strange Lady in Town**
Frankie Laine

10 **Ev'ry Day of My Life**
Malcolm Vaughan

The auction for Elvis Presley's contract ends on the 22nd with success for RCA, who pay Sam Phillips' Sun Records $25,000 and Hi-Lo Music $10,000. Everyone is happy. Phillips invests his cut in the new Holiday Inn chain, which proves an even better bet than Elvis. Colonel Parker, by masterminding the deal, has made himself indispensable. RCA have acquired what is virtually a licence to print money. Elvis buys another Cadillac.

In another important deal Leiber and Stoller sign up as independent producers with Atlantic and head for New York, taking half of the Robins group with them to form the nucleus of the Coasters. Between them they'll have a string of classic hits over the next five years.

In Nashville, the two sons of Knoxville radio performers Ike and Margaret Everly make their first recordings. Don is 18, Phil 16. They cut four songs in 22 minutes.

On *The Ed Sullivan Show* there is a 15-minute R&B segment. One of the four performers is Bo Diddley, who Sullivan wants to sing 'Sixteen Tons', the current Tennessee Ernie Ford hit. Diddley claims not to know it, is extensively coached, then plays his own 'Bo Diddley' anyway when showtime comes around. Sullivan is apparently 'more surprised than pleased'.

Billboard publishes its first Top 100 chart and announces the results of its annual DJ poll. Fats Domino is the top R&B artist, Chuck Berry the most promising R&B newcomer. Elvis is still only the most promising Country and Western singer.

USA

1 **Autumn Leaves**
Roger Williams

2 **Love is a Many-Splendored Thing**
The Four Aces

3 **Yellow Rose of Texas**
Mitch Miller

4 **Moments to Remember**
Four Lads

5 **Shifting Whispering Sands**
Billy Vaughn

6 **Black Denim Trousers**
Cheers

7 **Bible Tells Me So**
Don Cornell

8 **Shifting Whispering Sands**
Rusty Draper

9 **Only You**
The Platters

10 **He**
Al Hibbler

UK

1 **The Man from Laramie**
Jimmy Young

2 **Yellow Rose of Texas**
Mitch Miller

3 **Blue Star**
Cyril Stapleton

4 **Rock around the Clock**
Bill Haley

5 **Hernando's Hideaway**
The Johnston Brothers

6 **Hey, There**
Rosemary Clooney

7 **Rose Marie**
Slim Whitman

8 **Cool Water**
Frankie Laine

9 **Hey, There**
Johnnie Ray

10 **The Breeze and I**
Caterina Valente

The Drifters, with lead singer Johnny Moore

Carl Perkins

Carl Perkins has now been with Sun for over a year, but Phillips has hitherto kept him on the country side of rockabilly. The resultant singles, all self-penned, have met with little success. Now, with Elvis gone to RCA, Phillips picks on Perkins to inherit the mantle, and encourages him to play up the rock'n'roll side of his music. As luck has it, Carl has just written the perfect song, based around an incident witnessed at a bandstand concert. 'Blue Suede Shoes' is cut on the 19th, and rush-released.

Two weeks earlier Sun has released Johnny Cash's 'Folsom Prison Blues', written by the singer after watching a movie about life inside. It reaches #5 on the country chart. Fourteen years later Cash will give a concert in Folsom, and the resultant live album will be a huge hit.

On the pop chart two of the decade's most successful black groups have entries. The Drifters' 'White Christmas' is their first, and climbs no higher than #80, but the Platters' 'The Great Pretender' is on its way to #1.

An interesting new release is 'Christmas Presents from Heaven' by a former boy preacher, Solomon Burke. Like all his gospel-influenced records of the '50s it will only sell in small numbers, but in the next decade Burke will become one of the mainstays of the Atlantic soul stable.

On Boxing Day Decca release Bill Haley and the Comets' 'See You Later, Alligator', which will become their second biggest American hit. In Britain, meanwhile, 'Rock around the Clock' has finally reached #1.

1956

1956 was the year it all came to fruition, particularly for one man. The move to RCA ushered in two years in which Elvis Presley could do no wrong: his records broke sales records, he started making movies, and he still managed to enrage one generation in a way which gave another its necessary sense of difference, of identity.

Chuck Berry and Little Richard consolidated their positions, and Fats Domino edged sideways from huge R&B success to mainstream fame. Others followed through the breach that this vanguard had made in the walls of tradition – Carl Perkins and

Gene Vincent foremost among them. The Everly Brothers, Buddy Holly and Eddie Cochran were all making their first steps towards stardom. Southerners almost to a man, each owed a debt of style to more than one of the strands running through pop, white country music and black rhythm, blues and gospel music.

Britain meanwhile was some way behind, still catching up with Bill Haley, welcoming Elvis Presley, conjuring a skiffle boom out of traditional jazz, and trying to manufacture its own rock'n'roll star in Tommy Steele.

Elvis Presley

With the New Year only a fortnight old, Bill Haley and the Comets become the first rock'n'roll act to make the Top 15 Album Chart with *Rock around the Clock*. The #1 all month is the soundtrack of the musical *Oklahoma*. This has taken over from Doris Day's *Love Me or Leave Me*, and will eventually give way to Dean Martin's *Memories are Made of This*.

On the 10th and 11th Elvis does his first sessions for RCA in New York, using more musicians than previously, and in particular drummer D. J. Fontana, who has become a regular member of his back-up band over the last few months of touring. The first number they cut is Ray Charles's 'I Got a Woman', the second a new song, 'Heartbreak Hotel'.

On the West Coast Leiber and Stoller supervise the first Coasters recording session in a Hollywood studio. The songs put down are 'Down in Mexico' and 'Turtle Dovin'', the former a further invitation to the pleasures of 'Smokey Joe's Cafe' territory, the latter an early indication that Leiber is switching his lyrical aim more towards the (overwhelmingly white) teenage audience.

In Nashville Buddy Holly's first recording session for Decca takes place on the 26th. Guitarist Sonny Curtis and bassist Don Guess are with him, but there's no Jerry Allison on drums, and neither the songs chosen (mostly his own) nor the sound achieved is too original.

In the UK 'Rock Island Line' by Lonnie Donegan enters the charts. Donegan is a banjo player for Chris Barber's jazz

USA

1 **Sixteen Tons**
Tennessee Ernie Ford

2 **Memories are Made of This**
Dean Martin

3 **I Hear You Knockin'**
Gale Storm

4 **He**
Al Hibbler

5 **Moments to Remember**
Four Lads

6 **Autumn Leaves**
Roger Williams

7 **Love and Marriage**
Frank Sinatra

8 **Nuttin' For Christmas**
Art Mooney–Barry Gordon

9 **Only You**
The Platters

10 **Love is a Many-Splendored Thing**
The Four Aces

UK

1 **Rock around the Clock**
Bill Haley

2 **Love is a Many Splendored Thing**
The Four Aces

3 **Rock-a-Beatin' Boogie**
Bill Haley

4 **Christmas Alphabet**
Dickie Valentine

5 **Meet Me On the Corner**
Max Bygraves

6 **Let's Have a Ding-Dong**
Winifred Atwell

7 **Ain't That a Shame**
Pat Boone

8 **Rock Island Line**
Lonnie Donegan

9 **The Ballad of Davy Crockett**
Bill Hayes

10 **Twenty Tiny Fingers**
The Stargazers

band, the song one showcased in the band's 'skiffle spot' and featured on their new 10-inch album. Its success will provide a launching-pad for both Donegan's solo career and the skiffle craze of the next two years.

Skiffle king Lonnie Donegan

Frankie Lymon (centre) and the Teenagers

USA

1 **Memories are Made of This**
Dean Martin

2 **Great Pretender**
The Platters

3 **Sixteen Tons**
Tennessee Ernie Ford

4 **Lisbon Antigua**
Nelson Riddle

5 **Rock and Roll Waltz**
Kay Starr

6 **Band of Gold**
Don Cherry

7 **See You Later, Alligator**
Bill Haley

8 **It's Almost Tomorrow**
Dream Weavers

9 **Dungaree Doll**
Eddie Fisher

10 **I Hear You Knockin'**
Gale Storm

UK

1 **Sixteen Tons**
Tennessee Ernie Ford

2 **The Ballad of Davy Crockett**
Bill Hayes

3 **Love is a Tender Trap**
Frank Sinatra

4 **Love and Marriage**
Frank Sinatra

5 **The Ballad of Davy Crockett**
Tennessee Ernie Ford

6 **Rock-a-Beatin' Boogie**
Bill Haley

7 **Rock Island Line**
Lonnie Donegan

8 **When You Lose the One You Love**
David Whitfield

9 **Love is a Many Splendored Thing**
The Four Aces

10 **Rock around the Clock**
Bill Haley

Frankie Lymon and the Teenagers' 'Why Do Fools Fall in Love' enters both the pop and R&B charts. It will be the biggest hit of the group's short but highly successful career, selling over 2 million. Frankie is only 13, the rest not much older; they are a prototypical black teenage group of the late '50s, occupying some mawkish middle ground between doo-wop and soul. Their 1956 song 'I'm Not a Juvenile Delinquent' will be enough to give delinquency a good name.

A more lasting star (and ex-delinquent) makes his recording debut. In January James Brown and his Famous Flames have been signed by Federal, and on 4 February they cut their first single, 'Please, Please, Please'. The record will sell well in Brown's South-eastern states home territory, but slowly elsewhere. It will be live performances that establish him as a star.

Two of the tracks recorded by the Everly Brothers in November are released as their first single – 'Keep A'Lovin' Me'/'The Sun Keeps Shining'. When it fails to sell Columbia will abandon them. Later in the year their father will look up old friend Chet Atkins in Nashville, and partly through his good offices the boys will get a songwriting contract with Acuff-Rose. Wesley Rose will become their manager.

Little Richard follows up 'Tutti Frutti' with another cleaned-up song, 'Long Tall Sally'. Screaming Jay Hawkins records the original 'I Put a Spell on You' in New York, and Jerry Lee Lewis and father, having financed the 300-mile trip through the sale of 33 dozen eggs, arrive in Memphis to demand an audition at Sun Records. Sam Phillips is away, but an assistant lets the determined Lewis in to make a demo.

23

Roy Orbison – without shades.
Inset: Carl Perkins

USA

1 **Lisbon Antigua**
Nelson Riddle

2 **Rock and Roll Waltz**
Kay Starr

3 **Great Pretender**
The Platters

4 **Memories are Made of This**
Dean Martin

5 **No, Not Much**
Four Lads

6 **See You Later, Alligator**
Bill Haley

7 **Poor People of Paris**
Les Baxter

8 **Band of Gold**
Don Cherry

9 **I'll Be Home/Tutti Frutti**
Pat Boone

10 **Sixteen Tons**
Tennessee Ernie Ford

UK

1 **Memories are Made of This**
Dean Martin

2 **Zambesi**
Lou Busch

3 **It's Almost Tomorrow**
The Dream Weavers

4 **Only You**
The Hilltoppers

5 **Rock and Roll Waltz**
Kay Starr

6 **Band of Gold**
Don Cherry

7 **Love is a Tender Trap**
Frank Sinatra

8 **Memories are Made of This**
Dave King

9 **Sixteen Tons**
Tennessee Ernie Ford

10 **Rock Island Line**
Lonnie Donegan

With 'Blue Suede Shoes' Carl Perkins enters both the pop and R&B charts, the first country star to do so. On the 22nd, however, tragedy strikes the singer. En route to New York for a prestigious appearance on *The Ed Sullivan Show* he is badly injured, and his brother Jay and his manager killed, in a Delaware car smash. Three months in hospital follow, and the momentum 'Blue Suede Shoes' has given his career is lost. As a guitarist and writer he still has much to offer, but later royalties from Beatles' recordings of his songs will far exceed the earnings from his own records.

Back in Memphis Sam Phillips has listened to the Jerry Lee Lewis demo, liked it, and invited him back to do some recording. The countryish 'Crazy Arms' is released as a first single – the pumping piano style is more distinctive than the restrained vocal.

Yet another new arrival on Sun's doorstep is young West Texan Roy Orbison. As a member of the Teen Kings he has cut several unsuccessful records at Norman Petty's Clovis studio, and one of them, a piece of rockabilly nonsense called 'Ooby Dooby', appeals to Phillips. He will get Orbison to re-record it, and the new record's relative success (#59) will encourage Phillips to demand more of the same, and to ignore the singer's desire to record some ballads.

Still in the South, an 11-year-old Brenda Lee makes her TV debut on Red Foley's *Ozark Jubilee*. Up north Bobby Darin makes his first record, a cover of Lonnie Donegan's UK hit 'Rock Island Line'. It doesn't sound as authentic as the Englishman's, which is now steadily climbing up the US chart.

USA

1 **Poor People of Paris**
Les Baxter

2 **Lisbon Antigua**
Nelson Riddle

3 **Rock and Roll Waltz**
Kay Starr

4 **No, Not Much**
Four Lads

5 **Hot Diggity/Juke Box Baby**
Perry Como

6 **I'll Be Home/Tutti Frutti**
Pat Boone

7 **Blue Suede Shoes**
Carl Perkins

8 **Why Do Fools Fall In Love**
Teenagers

9 **Heartbreak Hotel/I was the One**
Elvis Presley

10 **Great Pretender**
The Platters

UK

1 **Poor People of Paris**
Winifred Atwell

2 **It's Almost Tomorrow**
The Dream Weavers

3 **Rock and Roll Waltz**
Kay Starr

4 **Zambesi**
Lou Busch

5 **Memories are Made of This**
Dave King

6 **Only You**
The Hilltoppers

7 **Memories are Made of This**
Dean Martin

8 **See You Later, Alligator**
Bill Haley

9 **Chain Gang**
Jimmy Young

10 **Great Pretender**
Jimmy Parkinson

Nat 'King' Cole with a surfeit of pipes

The top-selling records in April, in both the US and UK, feature versions of the instrumental 'Poor People of Paris', but in most other respects it's Elvis Presley's month. In the first week an estimated one in four Americans see him on Milton Berle's TV show; in the last, 'Heartbreak Hotel' reaches #1 and passes the million sales mark. Equally welcoming, but rather more ominously for the future of rock'n'roll, Elvis is given his first movie contract and plays his first dates in Las Vegas.

Two further signs of the music's expanding frontiers: on the 7th CBS Radio go nationwide with Alan Freed's *Rock'n'Roll Dance Party*, and on the 16th two tracks from Buddy Holly's first Nashville session are released. The songs ('Blue Days, Black Nights' and 'Love me') are mediocre, the arrangement lacks any rhythmic drive, and the single will flop. But it's a lesson learned – Holly will bring his own drummer and ideas to the next session.

Down South the progressives have other problems. As a sign of battles still to be fought in that rough terrain where music and politics meet, on the 10th Nat 'King' Cole is viciously assaulted in Birmingham, Alabama. Six men rush the stage during his second number, knock him backwards so that his head hits a piano stool, and then drag him down into the auditorium before the police manage to intervene. One of the assailants is a director of the White Citizens' Council, a group endeavouring to support racial segregation by boycotting 'bop and Negro music'. The audience, needless to say, is 100 per cent white.

USA

1 **Heartbreak Hotel/I was the One**
Elvis Presley
2 **Hot Diggity/Juke Box Baby**
Perry Como
3 **Poor People of Paris**
Les Baxter
4 **Blue Suede Shoes**
Carl Perkins
5 **Lisbon Antigua**
Nelson Riddle
6 **Why Do Fools Fall in Love**
Teenagers
7 **Moonglow and Theme from 'Picnic'**
Morris Stoloff
8 **Magic Touch**
The Platters
9 **Rock Island Line**
Lonnie Donegan
10 **A Tear Fell/Bo Weevil**
Teresa Brewer

UK

1 **Poor People of Paris**
Winifred Atwell
2 **No Other Love**
Ronnie Hilton
3 **It's Almost Tomorrow**
The Dream Weavers
4 **A Tear Fell**
Teresa Brewer
5 **Rock and Roll Waltz**
Kay Starr
6 **Only You**
The Hilltoppers
7 **My September Love**
David Whitfield
8 **Main Title**
Billy May
9 **Theme from the Threepenny Opera**
Dick Hyman
10 **I'll be Home**
Pat Boone

On the 2nd, for the first time ever, the same five records hold positions in both pop and R&B Top Tens. 'Heartbreak Hotel' and 'Blue Suede Shoes' are also #1 and #2 in the Country and Western chart. The old boundaries are breaking down.

So far the British experience of this revolution hasn't gone much further than Bill Haley, but help is on the way. Alan Freed's two-hour show *Jamboree* takes over Saturday evenings on Radio Luxemburg, and 'Heartbreak Hotel' begins climbing the UK chart. On a different cultural level, but with much the same targets in mind, John Osborne's play *Look Back in Anger* premières in London.

Lonnie Donegan is taking his music back across the Atlantic, starting a month-long US tour to build on the American success of 'Rock Island Line'. In Britain the follow-up 'Lost John'/'Stewball' is on its way to #2.

Brenda Lee, having followed her March TV debut with appearances on the Perry Como and Ed Sullivan shows, signs a recording contract with Decca. Her first release, an energetic rendition of Hank Williams' 'Jambalaya' complete with wildly rocking sax, has some success on the country charts, but surprisingly fails to cross over.

In New York Johnny Burnette and the Rock'n'Roll Trio (brother Dorsey Burnette on bass and friend Paul Burlison on guitar) make their first single 'Tear It Up' for Coral, having won the label's attention by winning a TV amateur hour three weeks running. Johnny has been a schoolmate of Elvis Presley's, and the band have already been rejected by Sun for sounding too much like him. Despite, or perhaps because of all this, the single is not a success.

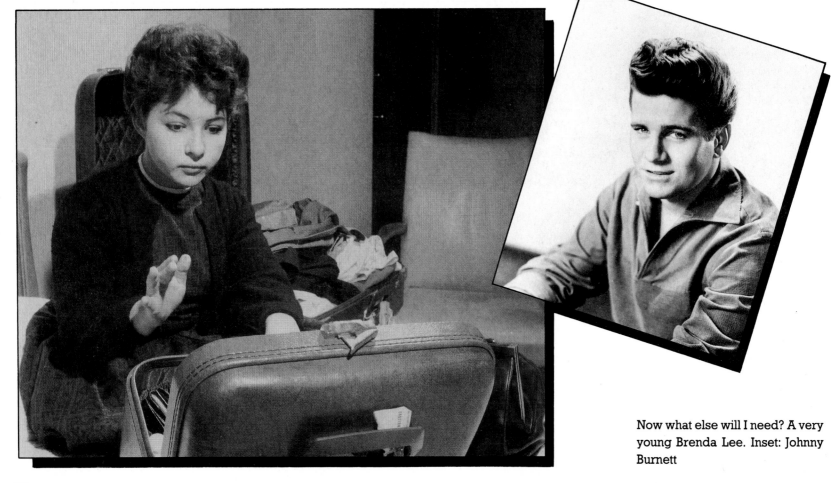

Now what else will I need? A very young Brenda Lee. Inset: Johnny Burnett

The Bluecaps manoeuvre Gene Vincent into position

Elvis Presley's ever-growing popularity has its problems – he's becoming a threat that Middle America has to take seriously. On the 5th he makes a second appearance on *The Milton Berle Show*, and provokes a wave of attacks from the critics. They are particularly incensed by the way he moves his whole body to the music, like 'the mating dance of an aborigine' as one puts it. A few days earlier *Time* has pronounced his diction 'poor' and summed up his appeal with the dreaded word 'sex'.

His success is also confusing the charts: 'Heartbreak Hotel' is now #1 on the pop, R&B and country lists. The record itself, needless to say, is both all of these and none of them.

Likewise 'Bee-Bop-A-Lula' by newcomers Gene Vincent and the Blue Caps, which is released on the 6th. Destined to be their biggest hit, reaching #7 in the US and #17 in Britain, the record is a further milestone in the distillation of a new music. There is nothing countryish about it, yet the vocal sound is unmistakably white, and though Cliff Gallup's guitar-playing owes everything to the blues, the whole performance, the enormous sense of compressed energy that Vincent evokes, makes 'Bee-Bop-A-Lula' prototypical rock'n'roll.

Chuck Berry is also both helping to create and moving towards the centre of this new mainstream. After two relative failures, his fourth single 'Roll over Beethoven' sets the pattern for two years of consistent success. The blues element has become almost subliminal, the guitar chimes rather than whines, the lyrics are squarely aimed, with wit, at white teen America.

USA

1 **Heartbreak Hotel/I was the One**
Elvis Presley

2 **Moonglow and Theme from 'Picnic'**
Morris Stoloff

3 **Hot Diggity/Juke Box Baby**
Perry Como

4 **Wayward Wind**
Gogi Grant

5 **Moonglow and Theme from 'Picnic'**
George Cates

6 **I'm in Love Again /My Blue Heaven**
Fats Domino

7 **Ivory Tower**
Cathie Carr

7 **Standing on the Corner /My Little Angel**
Four Lads

9 **Blue Suede Shoes**
Carl Perkins

10 **Magic Touch**
The Platters

UK

1 **No Other Love**
Ronnie Hilton

2 **A Tear Fell**
Teresa Brewer

3 **I'll be Home**
Pat Boone

4 **Lost John**
Lonnie Donegan

5 **My September Love**
David Whitfield

5 **Heartbreak Hotel**
Elvis Presley

7 **Poor People of Paris**
Winifred Atwell

8 **The Happy Whistler**
Don Robertson

9 **Main Title**
Billy May

10 **Rock and Roll Waltz**
Kay Starr

On the 1st Elvis Presley appears dressed in tails on *The Steve Allen Show*, and sings 'Hound Dog' to a real live basset hound. There are no hip movements. Next day teenagers picket the TV studio demanding 'the real Elvis'.

He's in the recording studio, together with the Jordanaires vocal group for the first time, putting down 'Anyway You Want Me', 'Don't Be Cruel' and 'Hound Dog'. The last-named requires 31 takes before Elvis is satisfied. 'Anyway You Want Me' is the heaviest music Elvis has yet created, with smouldering vocal and guitar.

In the UK Frankie Lymon and the Teenagers hit #1 with 'Why Do Fools Fall in Love' and Gene Vincent's 'Bee-Bop-A-Lula' enters the chart. The movie *Rock around the Clock* has arrived at last, drawing huge crowds. Buddy Holly's first single is released without success.

Holly and band are back in the Nashville studio, this time with friend and drummer Jerry Allison to provide a much crisper rhythm. The others have learned a lot themselves over the last six months – the guitar work from both Holly and Curtis is fresher, and so are Holly's vocals. One of the songs they record, its hook taken from John Wayne's oft-uttered line in *The Searchers*, is 'That'll be the Day'.

Decca are not impressed by it, or any of the other recorded songs, and proceed to sit on them. In September a frustrated Holly and Allison will decide to try Norman Petty's Clovis studio in New Mexico.

USA

1 **Wayward Wind**
   Gogi Grant

2 **Moonglow and Theme from 'Picnic'**
   Morris Stoloff

3 **I Almost Lost My Mind**
   Pat Boone

4 **Standing on the Corner/My Little Angel**
   Four Lads

5 **I'm in Love Again/My Blue Heaven**
   Fats Domino

6 **I Want You, I Need You, I Love You/My Baby Left Me**
   Elvis Presley

7 **More/Glendora**
   Perry Como

8 **Heartbreak Hotel/I was the One**
   Elvis Presley

9 **Ivory Tower**
   Cathie Carr

10 **On the Street Where You Live**
   Vic Damone

UK

1 **I'll Be Home**
   Pat Boone

2 **Lost John**
   Lonnie Donegan

3 **All Star Hit Parade**
   Various Artists

4 **Heartbreak Hotel**
   Elvis Presley

5 **Hot Diggity**
   Perry Como

6 **Saints Rock and Roll**
   Bill Haley

7 **Bluebottle Blues**
   The Goons

8 **Experiments with Mice**
   Johnny Dankworth

9 **Wayward Wind**
   Gogi Grant

10 **No Other Love**
   Ronnie Hilton

Buddy Holly, with and without Crickets

London has its first rock'n'roll club, the Studio 51 on Great Newport Street in Soho. Rory Blackwell's Rock 'n' Rollers are the resident live band, and one of the first – if not *the* first – British rock'n'roll groups. Tony Crombie's Rockets are formed days later. Both bands are Bill Haley and the Comets clones, with heavy reliance on sax and piano.

In the States Elvis Presley is now receiving 3,000 fan letters a week, and 'Hound Dog' is the fastest-selling record in American history. With this musical bandwagon rolling unstoppably onward, he starts work on his first film, *The Reno Brothers*. A Western set in the aftermath of the Civil War, the story has been changed to fit him, and the title soon follows suit, becoming *Love Me Tender* after one of the songs.

It's not a bad film, and the singer's performance is better than most people expect. The role itself is interesting: Elvis plays the youngest brother of three returning soldiers, and much of the plot relies, somewhat unbelievably, on his wife's preference for Richard Egan. Needless to say, Elvis makes the final noble sacrifice.

The Five Satins' 'In the Still of the Night' is a notable entry on the R&B charts. Written during a long night of guard duty in the Far East and recorded on a two-track in a church basement, it will sell well in excess of a million over the next few years. Many aficinados will come to regard it as the best doo-wop single of all time.

USA

1 **I Want You, I Need You, I Love You/My Baby Left Me**
Elvis Presley
2 **Wayward Wind**
Gogi Grant
3 **I Almost Lost My Mind**
Pat Boone
4 **My Prayer/Heaven On Earth**
Platters
5 **More/Glendora**
Perry Como
6 **Whatever Will Be, Will Be**
Doris Day
7 **Be-Bop-A-Lula**
Gene Vincent
8 **I'm in Love Again/My Blue Heaven**
Fats Domino
9 **Allegheny Moon**
Patti Page
10 **Born to Be with You**
The Chordettes

UK

1 **Why Do Fools Fall in Love**
Frankie Lymon and The Teenagers
2 **Whatever Will Be Will Be**
Doris Day
3 **A Sweet Old Fashioned Girl**
Teresa Brewer
4 **I'll be Home**
Pat Boone
5 **Walk Hand in Hand**
Tony Martin
6 **Bluebottle Blues**
The Goons
7 **Mountain Greenery**
Mel Torme
8 **All Star Hit Parade**
Various Artists
9 **Wayward Wind**
Tex Ritter
10 **Wayward Wind**
Gogi Grant

The Five Satins

Fats Domino's 'Blueberry Hill' enters the pop charts on its way to #2. The New Orleans singer-pianist has been having R&B hits (mostly written by him and band-leader Dave Bartholomew) since his first million-seller 'The Fat Man' in 1949, and he will carry on having rock'n'roll hits until the early '60s, accumulating 15 gold records in the process and outselling everyone bar Elvis Presley and the Beatles before or since.

On the 9th Elvis is making the first of three appearances on *The Ed Sullivan Show*. Sullivan has sworn never to have him on, but a marked rise in competitor Steve Allen's audiences forces a re-think. One of the songs Elvis performs is 'Love Me Tender', and next day shops are deluged with requests for the record. RCA bring forward the release schedule.

In Los Angeles, suburban teenager Eddie Cochran, after splitting up with friend Hank (with whom he has made several unsuccessful hillbilly records), joins forces with a new partner, Jerry Capehart. Together they write a song called 'Skinny Jim', and Cochran records it. This also fails to score, but the twosome start hawking it round other record companies as a demo.

In the same city 15-year-old Paul Anka manages to cut his first record, 'I Confess', while staying with his uncle for the summer vacation. Its release won't start a rush on the record stores, but by that time Anka, back at school in Ottawa, will have something else instead on his mind – the family's 18-year-old babysitter – Diana.

The boy can't help it – Eddie Cochran

USA

1 **Hound Dog/Don't Be Cruel**
Elvis Presley

2 **My Prayer/Heaven on Earth**
The Platters

3 **Whatever Will Be, Will Be**
Doris Day

4 **Flying Saucer**
Buchanan and Goodman

5 **Canadian Sunset**
Hugo Winterhalter

6 **Allegheny Moon**
Patti Page

7 **I Want You, I Need You, I Love You**
Elvis Presley

8 **Be-Bop-A-Lula**
Gene Vincent

9 **Almost Lost My Mind**
Pat Boone

10 **Tonight You Belong to Me**
Patience and Prudence

UK

1 **Whatever Will Be Will Be**
Doris Day

2 **Why Do Fools Fall in Love**
Frankie Lymon and The Teenagers

3 **A Sweet Old Fashioned Girl**
Teresa Brewer

4 **Rockin' through the Rye**
Bill Haley

5 **Walk Hand in Hand**
Tony Martin

6 **Mountain Greenery**
Mel Torme

7 **I Almost Lost My Mind**
Pat Boone

8 **Wayward Wind**
Tex Ritter

9 **Heartbreak Hotel**
Elvis Presley

9 **Serenade**
Slim Whitman

USA

1 **Don't Be Cruel/Hound Dog**
Elvis Presley

2 **My Prayer/Heaven on Earth**
The Platters

3 **Canadian Sunset**
Hugo Winterhalter
/Eddie Heywood

4 **Whatever Will Be, Will Be**
Doris Day

5 **Honky Tonk**
Bill Doggett

6 **Tonight You Belong to Me**
Patience and Prudence

7 **Fool**
Sanford Clark

8 **Just Walking In The Rain**
Johnnie Ray

9 **Allegheny Moon**
Patti Page

10 **Canadian Sunset**
Andy Williams

UK

1 **Lay Down Your Arms**
Anne Shelton

2 **Woman in Love**
Frankie Laine

3 **Whatever Will Be Will Be**
Doris Day

4 **Hound Dog**
Elvis Presley

5 **Giddy up a Ding-Dong**
Freddie Bell
and The Bell Boys

6 **Rockin' through the Rye**
Bill Haley

7 **Ying Tong Song**
The Goons

8 **The Great Pretender**
The Platters

9 **Only You**
The Platters

10 **Rock around the Clock**
Bill Haley

In Britain Bill Haley has five records in the Top Twenty, largely thanks to the *Rock around the Clock* movie, but the rest of the charts have a more traditional look. Anne Shelton's 'Lay Down Your Arms', which has taken over the top spot from Doris Day's 'Whatever Will Be, Will Be' in mid-September, is usurped four weeks later by Frankie Laine's 'Woman in Love'. Johnnie Ray's 'Just Walkin' in the Rain' comes in at #14, also en route to #1. Only Elvis Presley, Gene Vincent and the Goons' 'Ying Tong Song' threaten to disturb the peace.

Plus one newcomer. Tommy Steele, a Bermondsey boy with a winning smile and not much musical talent, has been given a three-month hype as the long-awaited British Elvis. He gets a first TV appearance on the 15th, and performs his first single, 'Rock with the Cavemen'. It enters the charts a week later.

In Hollywood the success of *Blackboard Jungle* and *Rock around the Clock* has not passed unnoticed, and several rock'n'roll movies are now on the drawing board. One, provisionally titled 'Do Re Mi', will see the light of day as *The Girl Can't Help It*.

Considered by most critics the best of the '50s rock'n'roll films, it will both boost the careers of stars Little Richard and Fats Domino, and provide other lesser mortals with their chance to break through into the limelight. One of those trawled up by the studio to provide authentic teen music is Eddie Cochran, who performs 'Twenty Flight Rock' in a three-minute cameo. Together with the 'Skinny Jim' demo it will be enough to land him a recording contract with Liberty.

**Britain's Elvis – Tommy Steele.
Inset: The Fat Man – Fats Domino**

November 1956

USA

1 **Don't Be Cruel/Hound Dog**
Elvis Presley

2 **Love Me Tender**
Elvis Presley

3 **Green Door**
Jim Lowe

4 **Honky Tonk**
Bill Doggett

5 **Just Walking In the Rain**
Johnnie Ray

6 **Canadian Sunset**
Hugo Winterhalter
/Eddie Heywood

7 **Tonight You Belong to Me**
Patience and Prudence

8 **Whatever Will Be, Will Be**
Doris Day

9 **Blueberry Hill**
Fats Domino

10 **Friendly Persuasion/Chains of Love**
Pat Boone

UK

1 **Woman in Love**
Frankie Laine

2 **Hound Dog**
Elvis Presley

3 **Just Walking in the Rain**
Johnnie Ray

4 **Lay Down Your Arms**
Anne Shelton

5 **Rockin' through the Rye**
Bill Haley

6 **My Prayer**
The Platters

7 **Giddy up a Ding-Dong**
Freddie Bell
and The Bell Boys

8 **More**
Jimmy Young

9 **When Mexico Gave up the Rhumba**
Mitchell Torok

10 **Rock around the clock**
Bill Haley

Johnny Cash has his first crossover success with the self-penned 'I Walk the Line'. The song has started off life as a slow ballad, and Cash has performed it like that on the influential *Louisiana Hayride* TV show, before Sam Phillips persuades him to speed it up for recording. Now, six months after release, it makes #17 on the pop chart, after several weeks at #2 on the country chart. Over the next 30 years Cash will carry on straddling the line, neither abandoning country music nor letting himself get trapped within its musical and thematic limitations.

The movie *Love Me Tender* is released to a mixed critical response, but Paramount are unlikely to be unduly concerned – the film recoups its cost in four days. The second album, simply titled *Elvis*, reaches #1 on the album charts.

Guy Mitchell's 'Singing the Blues' enters the single charts. He's been having hits since 1950, mostly by turning folk songs into cheerful singalong pop. This one will reach #1 on both sides of the Atlantic, despite a cover version from Tommy Steele.

After a sustained campaign by knowledgeable British fans a Little Richard record is finally released in the UK – the current US success 'Rip It Up'. Unfortunately a cover version appears almost immediately, by the man *New Musical Express* readers have just voted the World's Most Outstanding Vocal Personality – Bill Haley.

The annual DJ poll in *Billboard* confirms what everyone knows – DJs are always the last people to spot a musical trend. Their favourite record is 'Moonglow and Theme from *Picnic*' by Morris Stoloff. 'Don't Be Cruel' comes seventeenth.

USA

1. **Love Me Tender**
   Elvis Presley
2. **Singing the Blues**
   Guy Mitchell
3. **Green Door**
   Jim Lowe
4. **Just Walking in the Rain**
   Johnnie Ray
5. **True Love**
   Bing Crosby and Grace Kelly
6. **Blueberry Hill**
   Fats Domino
7. **Don't Be Cruel/Hound Dog**
   Elvis Presley
8. **Honky Tonk**
   Bill Doggett
9. **Hey, Jealous Lover**
   Frank Sinatra
10. **Friendly Persuasion/Chains of Love**
    Pat Boone

UK

1. **Just Walking in the Rain**
   Johnnie Ray
2. **Woman in Love**
   Frankie Laine
3. **Green Door**
   Frankie Vaughan
4. **My Prayer**
   The Platters
5. **Rip It Up**
   Little Richard
6. **St Theresa of the Roses**
   Malcolm Vaughan
7. **More**
   Perry Como
8. **Hound Dog**
   Elvis Presley
9. **Blue Moon (E.P.)**
   Elvis Presley
10. **When Mexico Gave up the Rhumba**
    Mitchell Torok

The year ends as it has begun, with Elvis's star firmly in the ascendant, although he has recently surrendered the #1 spot to Guy Mitchell after a phenomenal 17-week occupancy, first with 'Hound Dog'/'Don't Be Cruel', and then with 'Love Me Tender'.

On the 4th he drops in on Sun's Memphis studio for old times' sake and finds Carl Perkins recording 'Matchbox' with Jerry Lee Lewis sitting in on piano. Johnny Cash, the fourth member of this alleged 'Million Dollar Quartet', is only there for a few minutes before his wife drags him off to the shops. The other three horse around with a few songs, and Sam Phillips has the presence of mind to keep the tapes rolling on posterity's behalf.

On the 5th Alan Freed's third rock'n'roll movie – the imaginatively titled *Rock, Rock, Rock* – opens with the usual roster of stars, which includes the still hitless Johnny Burnette Trio and the still invisible Connie Francis, whose first claim to fame is dubbing in Tuesday Weld's singing part in the film.

Mickey and Sylvia, a singing and guitar-playing duo, have their biggest hit with 'Love is Strange'. Co-written by Mickey, it will reach #2 and #13 on the R&B and pop charts respectively. Lonnie Donegan's cover of the song will back his UK #1 'Cumberland Gap', and in the next few years Buddy Holly and the Everly Brothers will both produce interesting versions.

In Britain Tommy Steele makes an acclaimed stage debut, and no one seems to notice that the latest single from the 'English Elvis Presley' ('Singing the Blues') hardly qualifies as rock'n'roll.

Mickey and Sylvia

1957

The tumultuous arrival of Jerry Lee Lewis notwithstanding, 1957 was the year that rock'n'roll began to lose its original cutting edge. Little Richard quit the scene late in the year, and Elvis would be spirited away by the Army early in 1958. But the loss of these two founding fathers was not the basic reason for the change, only an exacerbating factor.

Rock'n'roll had always been as much about attitude as mere sound, and attitudes were softening with familiarity. White teenage music was now an established market, and one that TV was eager to exploit. In the USA *American Bandstand*, in Britain *6.5 Special*, began their influential careers, promoting the teenage way of life as part of the entertainment industry. The singers wore suits, and their songs wore concerns, even targets, that were now safe and predictable.

The music was growing softer too, as the heavy beat crossbred with an older pop tradition that relied more on tunes. Performers like the Everly Brothers, Buddy Holly and Ricky Nelson had none of the aggression of their immediate forebears. A new, more equal balance was being reached between rhythm and melody.

Buddy Holly

The year begins with Guy Mitchell's 'Singing the Blues' #1 on both sides of the Atlantic, and Fats Domino succeeding himself at the top of the R&B chart. A new entry on the pop chart is Harry Belafonte's 'Banana Boat Song (Day-O)'.

The song comes from his album *Calypso*, which has spent most of the last six months at the top of the album charts. Belafonte, a 29-year-old New Yorker with strong Jamaican connections, has tried jazz singing, acting and running a restaurant in Greenwich Village, before finding a profitable and important niche as a popularizer of (mostly Caribbean) folk music. *Calypso* will ship a million copies over the next few years – incredible sales for an album in the '50s – and Belafonte's success will both influence and open the way for groups like the Kingston Trio, whose own success will prove a major factor in the folk revival of the early '60s.

The UK's first real rock'n'roll TV show begins on New

USA

1 **Singing the Blues**
Guy Mitchell

2 **Love Me Tender**
Elvis Presley

3 **Green Door**
Jim Lowe

4 **Blueberry Hill**
Fats Domino

5 **True Love**
Bing Crosby and Grace Kelly

6 **Just Walking in the Rain**
Johnnie Ray

7 **Love Me**
Elvis Presley

8 **Rose And a Baby Ruth**
George Hamilton IV

9 **Banana Boat Song**
Tarriers

10 **Rock-a-Bye Your Baby**
Jerry Lewis

UK

1 **Singing the Blues**
Guy Mitchell

2 **Just Walking in the Rain**
Johnnie Ray

3 **Green Door**
Frankie Vaughan

4 **Singing the Blues**
Tommy Steele

4 **St Theresa of the Roses**
Malcolm Vaughan

6 **Rip It Up**
Little Richard

7 **True Love**
Bing Crosby and Grace Kelly

7 **Cindy, Oh Cindy**
Eddie Fisher

9 **Hound Dog**
Elvis Presley

10 **My Prayer**
The Platters

Two men possessed: (left) Harry Belafonte and (right) Jerry Lee Lewis

Year's Day. ITV's *Cool for Cats* is fronted by Kent Walton; it features records rather than live performances and studio dancers rather than the teenage public. In Liverpool the Cavern Club opens, but only, as yet, for jazz and a little skiffle.

On the 8th, his 22nd birthday, Elvis takes his US Army medical examination. Most of the month is spent working on his first Hal Wallis film, *Loving You*, but time is found for a third and last appearance on *The Ed Sullivan Show*. Elvis sings seven songs, but is shown only from the waist up during the uptempo ones.

35

USA

1 **Singing the Blues**
Guy Mitchell

2 **Young Love**
Sonny James

3 **Don't Forbid Me/Anastasia**
Pat Boone

4 **Young Love**
Tab Hunter

5 **Moonlight Gambler**
Frankie Laine

6 **Banana Boat Song**
Tarriers

7 **Blueberry Hill**
Fats Domino

8 **Green Door**
Jim Lowe

9 **Banana Boat Song**
Harry Belafonte

10 **Love Me Tender**
Elvis Presley

some lead guitar) cut their first tracks under Norman Petty's supervision. One of the new recordings is a harder, crisper version of the song they recorded six months previously in Decca's Nashville studio, 'That'll be the Day.'

The BBC's answer to *Cool for Cats* appears. *6.5 Special* is fronted by Pete Murray and Josephine Douglas, goes out on Saturday evenings, and does have live performances and dancing teenagers. It will be the model for most British pop TV over the next ten years.

Back in the States, Patsy Cline has her first crossover hit with 'Walking after Midnight', the Del-Vikings enter the charts with what will be their biggest success, 'Come Go with Me', and in a small club in deepest Arkansas Jerry Lee Lewis starts playing round with the words of a favourite song – 'Whole Lotta Shakin' Goin' On'.

UK

1 **Garden of Eden**
Frankie Vaughan

2 **Singing the Blues**
Guy Mitchell

3 **Singing the Blues**
Tommy Steele

4 **Friendly Persuasion**
Pat Boone

5 **True Love**
Bing Crosby and Grace Kelly

6 **St Theresa of the Roses**
Malcolm Vaughan

7 **Blueberry Hill**
Fats Domino

8 **Don't You Rock Me Daddy-O**
Lonnie Donegan

9 **Moonlight Gambler**
Frankie Laine

10 **Hound Dog**
Elvis Presley

In Los Angeles, between the 12th and 15th, the Coasters record four songs under Leiber and Stoller's direction. Two of them, both written by the producers, will make up their first million-selling single – 'Young Blood'/ 'Searchin''. The latter has the hero searching for his girl, and comparing himself to just about every American cultural hero he can think of in the process. 'Young Blood' has its protagonist drooling over a young girl, following her home and confronting her irate father. Both songs are specifically teenage dramas, written and performed as witty rock'n'roll.

They also represent something more. In pulling together the threads of different popular musics Leiber and Stoller are pulling back a musical curtain, revealing the artistic possibilities inherent in the new medium.

In Clovis, Buddy Holly and his band (now minus Sonny Curtis, squeezed out by Holly's desire to play at least

Four cool cats:
The Coasters

An editorial in *Cashbox* declares that original rock'n'roll is giving way to 'a softer version with emphasis on melody and lyric'. The initial impact of the 'big beat' has worn away, and kids are turning 'to the more melodic tune, the less raucous sound...'.

In the charts there is much to support this view. 'Young Love', a song with only an insistent rhythm and explicitly teenage sentiments to distinguish it from much of the last 50 years' popular music, is #1 in both the US and UK. Future #1 'Party Doll' by Buddy Knox and new entry 'Twenty Flight Rock' by Eddie Cochran are both to some extent prettified rock'n'roll. The Diamonds' 'Little Darlin'', on its way to #2, shows white groups can now doo-wop with a style once considered a purely black prerogative. And as if to confirm civilization's triumph over the rock'n'roll frontier, its number one hero goes into the property market and buys Graceland.

On the other side of the argument, Fats Domino hits #1 on the R&B chart with 'I'm Walkin'', taking over from his own 'Blue Monday'. By mid-April he will have held the #1 spot on the chart for 21 consecutive weeks.

Chess Records have two important releases. Chuck Berry's 'School Day' continues his run of teen anthems, and Muddy Waters' 'I Got My Mojo Workin'' continues his run of classic R&B hits. The recordings made by Waters' City Blues Band through the following decade will be a major influence in the white R&B movement of the mid-'60s.

Fats Domino

USA

1. **Too Much**
   Elvis Presley
2. **Young Love**
   Tab Hunter
3. **Don't Forbid Me/Anastasia**
   Pat Boone
4. **Young Love**
   Sonny James
5. **Banana Boat Song**
   Harry Belafonte
6. **Singing the Blues**
   Guy Mitchell
7. **Banana Boat Song**
   Tarriers
8. **Moonlight Gambler**
   Frankie Laine
9. **Blue Monday**
   Fats Domino
10. **Marianne**
    Terry Gilkyson

UK

1. **Young Love**
   Tab Hunter
2. **Don't Forbid Me**
   Pat Boone
3. **Knee Deep in the Blues**
   Guy Mitchell
4. **Garden of Eden**
   Frankie Vaughan
5. **Singing the Blues**
   Guy Mitchell
6. **Don't You Rock Me Daddy-O**
   Lonnie Donegan
7. **True Love**
   Bing Crosby and Grace Kelly
8. **Long Tall Sally**
   Little Richard
9. **Friendly Persuasion**
   Pat Boone
10. **Young Love**
    Sonny James

USA

1 **Party Doll**
Buddy Knox

2 **Round and Round**
Perry Como

3 **Butterfly**
Charlie Gracie

4 **Butterfly**
Andy Williams

5 **Teen-age Crush**
Tommy Sands

6 **I'm Walkin'**
Fats Domino

7 **Little Darlin'**
Diamonds

8 **Young Love**
Tab Hunter

9 **Marianne**
Terry Gilkyson

10 **Why, Baby, Why?**
Pat Boone

As if determined to prove the March editorial in *Cashbox* correct, Andy Williams' 'Butterfly' takes over from Elvis's 'All Shook Up' at US #1.

In New York the young Paul Anka is banging on record company doors, and two of the month's debut releases look forward to success stories built more on melody than the big beat.

Manager Wesley Rose has persuaded Archie Bleyer at Cadence that the Everly Brothers are the act he's been looking for, but Bleyer doesn't think much of their songs, and suggests they record one that's already been rejected by 30 acts – 'Bye Bye Love' by Boudleaux and Felice Bryant. The brothers cut it at Nashville's RCA Studio, with Chet Atkins supervising, and between them they conjure up the perfect merger of

The Everly Brothers – Phil (left) and Don (right)

rock'n'roll and country styles – pure harmony singing over acoustic strumming and a rock'n'roll beat.

Ricky Nelson is also from a showbiz family – he's been growing up on TV as part of his parents' *Adventures of Ozzie and Harriet* show – but he's more than just a manufactured image. True, he's good-looking, he's not much of a musician and he doesn't write his own songs, but there's more to Nelson than a Fabian or Frankie Avalon. His voice, equally at home on ballads and uptempo numbers, makes up in tone what it lacks in range, and either he or someone close to him will show near-

UK

1 **Young Love**
Tab Hunter

2 **Don't Forbid Me**
Pat Boone

3 **Long Tall Sally**
Little Richard

4 **Knee Deep in the Blues**
Guy Mitchell

5 **Banana Boat Song**
Harry Belafonte

6 **Cumberland Gap**
Lonnie Donegan

7 **Don't You Rock Me Daddy-O**
Lonnie Donegan

8 **Look Homeward Angel**
Johnnie Ray

9 **Cumberland Gap**
The Vipers

10 **Only You**
The Platters

impeccable taste in their choice of material over the next five years. The first single, 'A Teenager's Romance'/'I'm Walkin'', will make #2 and #17.

On the '6.5 Special' set

Chuck Berry's 'School Day' spends a week at #1 on the R&B chart, then makes way for a 13-week

USA

1 **All Shook Up**
Elvis Presley

2 **Little Darlin'**
The Diamonds

3 **Round and Round**
Perry Como

4 **Party Doll**
Buddy Knox

5 **Come Go with Me**
Del Vikings

6 **Gone**
Ferlin Husky

7 **I'm Walkin'**
Fats Domino

8 **School Day**
Chuck Berry

9 **Why, Baby, Why?**
Pat Boone

10 **Butterfly**
Andy Williams

run by the Coasters' 'Searchin''/'Young Blood'. Pat Boone's 'Love Letters in the Sand' enters the pop charts en route to becoming his fourth #1 in two years. The Crickets' 'That'll be the Day' is released on Brunswick, but doesn't attract much immediate attention.

In England the skiffle craze, encouraged by the *6.5 Special* TV show and its national skiffle contest, is now in full swing. Lonnie Donegan is at #1 with 'Cumberland Gap', and there are three other skiffle records in the Top Twenty. One is 'Maggie May' by the Vipers, a group which includes two future members of the Shadows, Jet Harris and Tony Meehan.

The main impact of the craze, though, will not be in record sales but in the encouragement it gives teenagers to do it themselves, to make their own music. One of the groups now introducing 'Cumberland Gap' to its repertoire is the Quarrymen, led by 16-year-old John Lennon.

An influential US album release is *Swinging Guitars* from Jorgen Ingmann. His twangy guitar sound looks forward to Duane Eddy and Hank B. Marvin; the album contains the original version of the Shadows' 1960 UK chart-topper 'Apache'.

Elvis, with writers Leiber and Stoller in attendance, records the songs for his latest

movie, *Jailhouse Rock*, and then spends most of the rest of the month on the Hollywood film set.

UK

1 **Cumberland Gap**
Lonnie Donegan

2 **Baby Baby**
Frankie Lymon
and The Teenagers

3 **Banana Boat Song**
Harry Belafonte

4 **Long Tall Sally**
Little Richard

5 **Rock-a-Billy**
Guy Mitchell

6 **Young Love**
Tab Hunter

7 **When I Fall in Love**
Nat 'King' Cole

8 **Butterfly**
Andy Williams

9 **Look Homeward Angel**
Johnnie Ray

10 **Ninety-Nine Ways**
Tab Hunter

USA

1 **All Shook Up**
Elvis Presley

2 **Love Letters in the Sand/Bernardine**
Pat Boone

3 **School Day**
Chuck Berry

4 **Little Darlin'**
The Diamonds

5 **White Sport Coat**
Marty Robbins

6 **So Rare**
Jimmy Dorsey

7 **I'm Walkin'/A Teenager's Romance**
Ricky Nelson

8 **Come Go with Me**
Del Vikings

9 **Gone**
Ferlin Husky

10 **Round and Round**
Perry Como

UK

1 **Butterfly**
Andy Williams

2 **Yes Tonight Josephine**
Johnnie Ray

3 **Rock-a-Billy**
Guy Mitchell

4 **When I Fall in Love**
Nat 'King' Cole

5 **I'll Take You Home Again Kathleen**
Slim Whitman

6 **Freight Train**
Chas McDevitt and Nancy Whiskey

7 **Baby Baby**
Frankie Lymon and The Teenagers

8 **Cumberland Gap**
The Vipers

9 **Cumberland Gap**
Lonnie Donegan

10 **Mr Wonderful**
Peggy Lee

On the 12th Jerry Lee Lewis's 'Whole Lotta Shakin' Goin' On' enters the country chart, on the 19th the pop chart. His first single has been restrained; this isn't. 'Whole Lotta Shakin'' is driven on by drumming, pushed forward, hauled back and rammed forward again by Lewis's pumping piano. The echoed vocal floats above it all, vaguely salacious, vaguely detached. In some way it seems the purest of all the rock'n'roll classics, celebrating only the power of its own music.

A song destined to inspire many covers, Dale Hawkins' 'Susie-Q', makes its chart debut. Hawkins will have a string of lesser hits over the next few years with his individual style of country raunch; lead guitarist James Burton will later provide inventive breaks on many of Ricky Nelson's hits, and feature on many country rock recordings of the late '60s and '70s.

Chuck Berry makes the UK chart for the first time with 'School Day', but it peaks at #24; only 'Sweet Little Sixteen' of his '50s records will scrape into the Top Twenty. His influence in England will be more keenly felt by fledgling musicians than the mass audience.

A sizeable portion of this is enjoying 'Rock across the Channel', continuous rock'n'roll by boat from Gravesend to Calais and back, featuring Rory Blackwell's band, Chas McDevitt's group and Terry Dene. The tickets are £2 each. The sea stays calm.

On dry land the skiffle craze shows no sign of abating. Lonnie Donegan fills the Albert Hall on the 9th, and his new single 'Gamblin' Man'/ 'Puttin' on the Style' charges up the chart.

(Above) Marty Robbins and
(below) Jerry Lee Lewis

Larry Williams

USA

1 **Love Letters in the Sand/Bernardine**
Pat Boone

2 **Bye Bye Love**
Everly Brothers

3 **So Rare**
Jimmy Dorsey

4 **Teenager's Romance /I'm Walkin'**
Ricky Nelson

5 **All Shook Up**
Elvis Presley

6 **Searchin'/Young Blood**
Coasters

7 **Dark Moon**
Gale Storm

8 **White Sport Coat**
Marty Robbins

9 **Start Movin'/Love Affair**
Sal Mineo

10 **Little Darlin'**
The Diamonds

UK

1 **Gambling Man**
Lonnie Donegan

2 **All Shook Up**
Elvis Presley

3 **Yes Tonight Josephine**
Johnnie Ray

4 **Little Darlin'**
The Diamonds

5 **Around the World**
Ronnie Hilton

6 **We Will Make Love**
Russ Hamilton

7 **When I Fall in Love**
Nat 'King' Cole

8 **Around the World**
Bing Crosby

9 **A White Sports Coat**
The King Brothers

10 **Mr Wonderful**
Peggy Lee

Elvis Presley continues to push all before him. 'All Shook Up' is his first British #1, taking over from Lonnie Donegan's 'Gamblin' Man' at the beginning of the month. He has already claimed the US #1 spot with two songs from the new movie, 'Teddy Bear'/'Loving You'. To complete the set, the month ends with the *Loving You* soundtrack atop the album chart.

On the 28th Jerry Lee Lewis makes his national TV debut on *The Steve Allen Show*. His act causes a sensation, and the mainly southern sales of 'Whole Lotta Shakin' Goin' On' become a national rush. By September it will be #3 on the pop chart, #1 on both country and R&B lists. If rock'n'roll is beginning to lose its vitality, this is the storm before the calm.

Larry Williams' 'Short Fat Fannie' enters both R&B and pop charts, the first of several huge successes on the former. Whereas the Coasters' 'Searchin' ' is packed with TV, movie and comic heroes, 'Short Fat Fannie' is full of references to other rock'n'roll songs. The music is becoming self-referential, a world of its own.

Rock'n'roll is becoming a serious business, a business to get serious about. The 'B' side of Williams' single, 'High School Dance', is written by a young LA hopeful named Sonny Bono. And away in distant Liverpool 14-year-old Paul McCartney attends a church picnic where 16-year-old John Lennon's Quarrymen are playing. He introduces himself to Lennon, and teaches him how to play 'Twenty Flight Rock' and 'Bee-Bop-A-Lula'.

On the 5th Dick Clark's Philadelphia TV show *Bandstand* goes national for the first time. Over the next few years *American Bandstand* will be the single most influential force in determining what the American public get to hear and see in the way of popular music. For those still in love with the earthier forms of rock'n'roll the influence will be mostly negative, as Clark will tend to promote clean-cut replicas of himself, suburban America's boys and girls next door.

One such is Paul Anka. 'Diana' hits #1 in both US and UK in the last week of the month, and will remain there for seven more in Britain. The first of three late '50s classics using the chords C/F/Am/G7 ('All I Have to Do is Dream' and 'Dream Lover' will follow), 'Diana' mixes energy, despair and wistful innocence into a potent cocktail of teenage angst.

The Everly Brothers are on *The Ed Sullivan Show*, singing 'Bye Bye Love' and its successor, 'Wake up Little Susie'. A risqué little tale of teenagers falling asleep in a bad movie and not making it home on time, the song might have caused problems for artists less blessed with such a spotless image.

The Crickets' 'That'll Be The Day', released back in May, finally enters the charts. Petty has decided to market Buddy Holly both in his own right and as part of the Crickets. The solo 'Words of Love' makes no impact, though it will later be recorded by the Beatles. The next pair – the Crickets' 'Oh Boy' and Holly's 'Peggy Sue' – will both be enormous hits.

USA

1 **Teddy Bear/Loving You**
Elvis Presley

2 **Love Letters in the Sand/Bernardine**
Pat Boone

3 **Bye Bye Love**
Everly Brothers

4 **So Rare**
Jimmy Dorsey

5 **Searchin'/Young Blood**
The Coasters

6 **It's You I Love /Valley of Tears**
Fats Domino

7 **Send For Me /My Personal Possession**
Nat 'King' Cole

8 **Old Cape Cod/Wondering**
Patti Page

9 **Over the Mountain**
Johnnie & Joe

10 **Dark Moon**
Gale Storm

UK

1 **All Shook Up**
Elvis Presley

2 **Teddy Bear**
Elvis Presley

3 **Gambling Man/Puttin' On the Style**
Lonnie Donegan

4 **We Will Make Love**
Russ Hamilton

5 **Little Darlin'**
The Diamonds

6 **Love Letters in the Sand**
Pat Boone

7 **Lucille**
Little Richard

8 **Around the World**
Ronnie Hilton

9 **Island in the Sun**
Harry Belafonte

10 **Yes Tonight Josephine**
Johnnie Ray

Waiting for the phone to ring – Dick Clark surveys his kingdom on 'American Bandstand'.

Most interesting release of the month is Jackie Wilson's 'Reet Petite'. Discovered by Johnny Otis at a 1951 talent show, Wilson replaced Clyde McPhatter as the Dominoes' lead singer in 1953, and had since built a reputation as one of the finest R&B vocalists around. 'Reet Petite', with its amazingly exuberant vocal gymnastics, will not be a huge American success in 1957, but for some reason British record-buyers love it. It will go to #6 on the UK chart in November and, more astonishingly, all the way to #1 when re-released 29 years later.

One of the song's writers is Berry Gordy Jr, until recently a part-time Ford assembly-line worker in the Motor City. A string of writing and production successes over the next few years will eventually encourage him to launch his own label – Tamla-Motown.

In New Orleans Malcolm John Rebennack – one of the few whites working as a session musician in the local scene – records his first single, 'Storm Warning'. In later years Rebennack will use local and psychedelic ingredients to cook up a strange musical brew under the name of Dr John the Night Tripper.

Gene Vincent's 'Lotta Lovin'' enters the charts, on its way to #13. Frankie Lymon, having split from The Teenagers and launched a solo career at the ripe old age of 15, releases his first solo single. It will flop, and so will its successors. Lymon will become one of the less-publicized rock'n'roll drug casualties of the late '60s.

Jackie Wilson, whose success with 'Reet Petite' will be echoed nearly three decades later.

USA

1 **Tammy**
Debbie Reynolds

2 **Teddy Bear/Loving You**
Elvis Presley

3 **Diana**
Paul Anka

4 **Searchin'/Young Blood**
Coasters

5 **Love Letters in the Sand/Bernardine**
Pat Boone

6 **Bye Bye Love**
Everly Brothers

7 **That'll be the Day**
The Crickets

8 **Rainbow**
Russ Hamilton

9 **Send For Me/My Personal Possession**
Nat 'King' Cole

10 **So Rare**
Jimmy Dorsey

UK

1 **Diana**
Paul Anka

2 **Love Letters in the Sand**
Pat Boone

3 **Last Train to San Fernando**
Johnny Duncan

4 **All Shook Up**
Elvis Presley

5 **Island in the Sun**
Harry Belafonte

6 **Water Water/Handful of Songs**
Tommy Steele

7 **Teddy Bear**
Elvis Presley

8 **Bye Bye Love**
The Everly Brothers

9 **With All My Heart**
Petula Clark

10 **Paralysed**
Elvis Presley

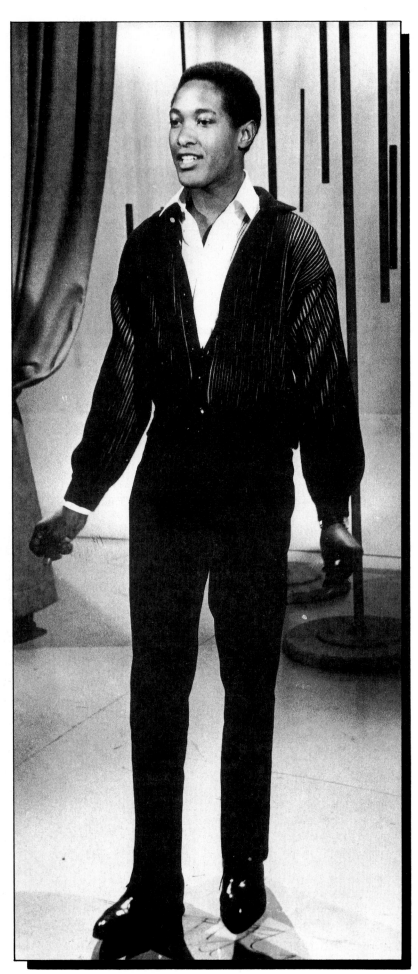

Sam Cooke – the voice of sweet soul music

USA

1 **That'll be the Day**
The Crickets

2 **Tammy**
Debbie Reynolds

3 **Diana**
Paul Anka

4 **Honeycomb**
Jimmy Rodgers

5 **Whole Lotta' Shakin' Goin' On**
Jerry Lee Lewis

6 **Teddy Bear/Loving You**
Elvis Presley

7 **Mr Lee**
The Bobbettes

8 **Rainbow**
Russ Hamilton

9 **In the Middle of an Island/I Am**
Tony Bennett

10 **Remember You're Mine/ There's a Gold Mine in the Sky**
Pat Boone

UK

1 **Diana**
Paul Anka

2 **Love Letters in the Sand**
Pat Boone

3 **Last Train to San Fernando**
Johnny Duncan

4 **Wanderin' Eyes**
Charlie Gracie

5 **Island in the Sun**
Harry Belafonte

6 **Tammy**
Debbie Reynolds

7 **Water Water/Handful of Songs**
Tommy Steele

8 **With All My Heart**
Petula Clark

9 **All Shook Up**
Elvis Presley

10 **That'll be the Day**
The Crickets

There are two pieces of bad news for America. The Russians are first in space with Sputnik, and on the 12th Little Richard announces he's quitting rock'n'roll. 'God doesn't like it,' he declares, midway through an Australian tour. Dared by one of his saxophonists to prove his faith, the singer chucks four diamond rings into Sydney Harbour. In January he will enrol at a religious college in Alabama, adding in further explanation that his prayers had extinguished a burning plane engine over the Philippines.

Jerry Lee Lewis is still keeping the other faith, recording his second and last classic, 'Great Balls of Fire', at the Sun studio in Memphis. He does have his doubts about the righteousness of the central image though, and starts arguing theology in the studio with Sam Phillips. Billy Lee Riley watches them both in amazement – 'Man alive!... let's cut it!'

A voice that many in later years will consider *the* soul voice makes its chart debut. Sam Cooke has been making gospel records at Specialty, but 'Bumps' Blackwell, producer and co-writer of many of Little Richard's hits for the label, sees a future for him in the pop market. When Blackwell leaves Specialty for Keen he takes Cooke with him. The second single, 'You Send Me', will reach #1, the first of 29 Top Forty entries over the next eight years.

Specialty, meanwhile, releases Larry Williams' follow-up to 'Short Fat Fannie' – the classic 'Bony Moronie'. Across the water Marty Wilde, one of the biggest pre-Beatles English stars, makes his TV debut on *Off the Record*.

USA

1 **Jailhouse Rock/Treat Me Nice**
Elvis Presley

2 **Wake up Little Susie**
Everly Brothers

3 **Honeycomb**
Jimmie Rodgers

4 **Tammy**
Debbie Reynolds

5 **Chances Are**
Johnny Mathis

6 **Be-Bop Baby/Have I Told You Lately That I Love You?**
Ricky Nelson

7 **Diana**
Paul Anka

8 **Happy, Happy Birthday, Baby**
Tune Weavers

9 **Keep a Knockin'**
Little Richard

10 **That'll be the Day**
The Crickets

UK

1 **That'll be the Day**
The Crickets

2 **Let's Have a Party**
Elvis Presley

3 **Tammy**
Debbie Reynolds

4 **Diana**
Paul Anka

5 **Remember You're Mine**
Pat Boone

6 **Man on Fire/Wanderin' Eyes**
Frankie Vaughan

7 **Be My Girl**
Jim Dale

8 **Whole Lotta Shakin' Goin' On**
Jerry Lee Lewis

9 **Love Letters in the Sand**
Pat Boone

10 **Wanderin' Eyes**
Charlie Gracie

In the first week of the month Elvis Presley has eight titles in the UK Top Thirty, an all-time record. In America advance orders for the forthcoming Christmas album have already topped half a million. The latest movie, *Jailhouse Rock*, has been on release since 21 October, complete with expected queues. The title song is #1 on both pop and R&B charts.

It's not the only connection between the two. On the 4th, for the first time, the top six records on the two charts are identical – 'Jailhouse Rock', 'Wake up Little Susie', 'You Send Me', the Rays' 'Silhouettes', Ricky Nelson's 'Be-Bop Baby' and Jimmie Rodgers' 'Honeycomb'. To complete the set, and further emphasize how the divisions between the different types of American popular music are breaking down, the top two on the country chart are also the same.

'The Majesty of Love', performed by ad hoc duet Marvin Rainwater and Connie Francis, provides her chart debut. Danny and the Juniors' 'At the Hop', a future #1, is released on ABC-Paramount, having already sold several thousand on a small Philadelphia label. Its title has been changed from 'Do the Bop' at Dick Clark's suggestion, giving the lie to those who claim TV presenters have no imagination.

In Britain the skiffle craze is drawing to a close. Lonnie Donegan is well enough established to survive in his own right, and will have continued success with a mixed bag of nouveau folk ('Grand Coulee Dam', 'Tom Dooley') and novelty/comedy records ('My Old Man's a Dustman', 'Does Your Chewing Gum Lose Its Flavour'). The other skiffle bands dissolve, scatter and reform, this time with amplifiers.

'Anyway you want me, that's how I will be.' Elvis on stage

It's a month for believing that the old rock'n'roll is dead. Ricky Nelson's latest single, 'Stood Up'/'Waitin' in School', provides him with his sixth and seventh Top Forty entries in seven months. His album *Ricky* will top the album charts for a week in January, making him the only rock'n'roll/pop star other than Elvis Presley to achieve this distinction in pre-Beatles years. Sam Cooke is at #1 with 'You Send Me'; 'Peggy Sue' and 'Oh Boy' are climbing the chart. It's all high-quality stuff, but not what many purists would call rock'n'roll.

To make matters worse, two more of the founding fathers will soon follow Little Richard into at least temporary eclipse. Jerry Lee Lewis takes 13-year-old cousin Myra to be his third wife, a choice that won't go down too well with either his British audience or Americans who think Dick Clark is cute. Elvis gets his Army call-up papers. He is ordered to report on 20 January for two years' service.

At least he'll be out of Middle America's hair. The Christmas album has raised a storm of protests, and been banned by many radio stations, simply because certain people can't seem to imagine religion and Elvis in the same breath without blowing a fuse.

In New York two schoolfriends record 'Hey School Girl' under the names Tom and Jerry. It gets into the lower half of the Hot One Hundred, but, after appearing on *American Bandstand* and making several more singles that do nothing, the twosome drift apart, only to reunite eight years later as Simon and Garfunkel.

Ricky Nelson on stage

USA

1 **Jailhouse Rock/Treat Me Nice**
Elvis Presley

2 **Wake up Little Susie**
Everly Brothers

3 **You Send Me/Summertime**
Sam Cooke

4 **Silhouettes**
The Rays

5 **Be-Bop Baby/Have I Told You Lately That I Love You?**
Ricky Nelson

6 **April Love/When the Swallows Come back to Caplstrano**
Pat Boone

7 **Chances Are /The Twelfth of Never**
Johnny Mathis

8 **My Special Angel**
Bobby Helms

9 **Raunchy**
Bill Justis

10 **Little Bitty Pretty One**
Thurston Harris

UK

1 **Mary's Boy Child**
Harry Belafonte

2 **Wake up Little Susie**
The Everly Brothers

3 **I Love You Baby**
Paul Anka

4 **Be My Girl**
Jim Dale

5 **Party**
Elvis Presley

6 **Ma He's Making Eyes at Me**
Johnny Otis Show

7 **Remember You're Mine**
Pat Boone

8 **Santa Bring Back My Baby To Me**
Elvis Presley

9 **Alone**
Petula Clark

10 **That'll be the Day**
The Crickets

1958

1958 was a watershed year, a year for taking stock after the creative explosion of 1955–7, for beginning the slow exploration of the possibilities that had been opened up. Rock'n'roll, in its narrower sense, was already a minority interest, one of several strands in the new mainstream. Teen-oriented lyrics and a rhythmic base were prerequisites, but beyond that anything went, fast or slow, instrumental or *a cappella*, romantic slop, hard-edged satire or verbal slapstick.

This was the year the North and West took over from the South, and the geographical shift coincided with a turn from music that burnt with conviction to music that was engineered to please. Bobby Darin started his journey through the available genres with success as his one guiding star, Phil Spector started his with the idea of music as primarily a matter of production. Eddie Cochran created teen anthems that lacked only spontaneity, Jan and Dean started making records in garages, and Connie Francis sang rhythmic ballads at all tempos. The British finally found their own Elvis in Cliff Richard.

Chuck Berry

January 1958

The first US #1 of the year is Danny and the Juniors' 'At the Hop', a frenetic, mindless and catchy slice of doo-wop with Jerry Lee Lewis-style piano. The song sounds like it has been written by Dick Clark's computer – pop as mere product. More depressing still for traditionalists, it tops the R&B chart too.

The Johnny Otis Show's 'Ma, He's Making Eyes at Me' gives way to 'Great Balls of Fire' at the top of the UK chart, but Jerry Lee Lewis only retains the position for a week – Elvis Presley comes straight in at #1 with 'Jailhouse Rock', the first time this has ever been done. The slow ballad 'Don't' will go to #1 in the US a few weeks later. His military

USA

1 **April Love/When the Swallows Come Back to Capistrano**
Pat Boone

2 **At the Hop**
Danny and The Juniors

3 **Jailhouse Rock/Treat Me Nice**
Elvis Presley

4 **Raunchy**
Bill Justis

5 **You Send Me/Summertime**
Sam Cooke

6 **Peggy Sue**
Buddy Holly

7 **Great Balls of Fire**
Jerry Lee Lewis

8 **Kisses Sweeter Than Wine**
Jimmie Rodgers

9 **Chances Are/The Twelfth of Never**
Johnny Mathis

10 **Rock and Roll Music**
Chuck Berry

induction has been deferred two months to allow him to finish filming *King Creole*.

In Los Angeles Eddie

UK

1 **Ma He's Making Eyes At Me**
Johnny Otis Show

2 **Mary's Boy Child**
Harry Belafonte

3 **Wake up Little Susie**
The Everly Brothers

4 **I Love You Baby**
Paul Anka

5 **Great Balls of Fire**
Jerry Lee Lewis

6 **My Special Angel**
Malcolm Vaughan

7 **Reet Petite**
Jackie Wilson

8 **All the Way**
Frank Sinatra

9 **Kisses Sweeter Than Wine**
Jimmy Rodgers

10 **Diana**
Paul Anka

Cochran, still searching for that elusive formula, goes against the trend, hardening his sound whilst everyone

else seems to be softening theirs. 'Jeannie Jeannie Jeannie' has a ferocious rhythm, explosive guitar break and Presleyish vocals. But it only scrapes to #86 in the US Hot One Hundred, and won't even be released in Britain until 18 months after the singer's death.

Liverpool-Irish crooner Michael Holliday releases a cover of Marty Robbins's US single 'The Story of My Life'. Robbins's version has only just made the Top Twenty in the US, but Holliday takes his laid-back interpretation to #1 in Britain. His is one of only five British records in the UK Top Twenty – a new state of American domination that will remain fairly constant until late 1962.

Danny and the Juniors in the movie 'Let's Rock!'

(Left) The young Berry Gordy Jnr and (right) Pat Boone

Chuck Berry's 'Sweet Little Sixteen' enters the pop chart on its way to #2. Perhaps his best

USA

1 **At the Hop**
Danny and The Juniors

2 **Get a Job**
The Silhouettes

3 **Don't/I Beg of You**
Elvis Presley

4 **Stood Up/Waitin' in School**
Ricky Nelson

5 **Sail Along Silvery Moon /Raunchy**
Billy Vaughn

6 **Peggy Sue**
Buddy Holly

7 **Great Balls of Fire**
Jerry Lee Lewis

8 **April Love/When the Swallows Come Back to Capistrano**
Pat Boone

9 **Sugartime**
McGuire Sisters

10 **The Stroll**
The Diamonds

teen anthem, it will be his biggest hit of the '50s. The litany of cities turns America into a continental dance floor and unites a nation of teenagers, at least in their imagination. Rebellion is rarely explicit in Berry's songs, but always implicit – in the war between the repression and expression there's no doubt where he stands.

The same could have been said of Little Richard before his sudden religious conversion, and it's still true of his music – 'Good Golly Miss Molly', on its way to #10, dares you to believe your luck in being alive.

The Silhouettes' 'Get a Job' is taking a rather more sanguine message to #1. The style is energetic doo-wop,

the lyrics tackle some realities of urban existence with a directness that is rare for the time. It elicits an answer record, the first from the Miracles. 'Got a Job' is written by Berry Gordy Jr, Smokey Robinson and Tyrone Carlo. It only makes a slight dent on the R&B chart.

The Royal Teens' novelty record 'Short Shorts' enters the pop charts on its way to #3. The record is instantly forgettable, but two members of the group have distinguished futures. Bob Gaudio will later join the Four Seasons, co-writing most of their famous hits. Fifteen-year-old Al Kooper will go on to session work, arranging, playing the keyboards on Dylan's classic albums *Highway 61 Revisited* and

Blonde on Blonde, and then taking a pivotal role in the formation of the group Blood, Sweat and Tears.

UK

1 **Jailhouse Rock**
Elvis Presley

2 **The Story of My Life**
Michael Holliday

3 **Great Balls of Fire**
Jerry Lee Lewis

4 **Oh Boy**
The Crickets

5 **All the Way**
Frank Sinatra

6 **Ma He's Making Eyes at Me**
Johnny Otis Show

7 **Peggy Sue**
Buddy Holly

8 **Kisses Sweeter Than Wine**
Jimmy Rodgers

9 **My Special Angel**
Malcolm Vaughan

10 **The Story of My Life**
Gary Miller

Without a Top Forty entry since 'Sitting in the Balcony', Eddie Cochran comes up with one of the great rock'n'roll classics – his and Jerry Capehart's 'Summertime Blues'. Cochran's gruff semi-spoken vocal sardonically recounts the joys of the long summer vacation – work, parents, etc – over acoustic power-chording and a choppy rhythm. The same musical recipe will be used for 'C'mon Everybody' later in the year, and both songs will be repeatedly revived in live performance over the next 20 years. The Who will make a ritual of closing their shows with 'Summertime Blues'.

Another important release, on the 9th, is Link Wray's innovative instrumental 'Rumble'. The title conjures up gangfights, and so does the guitar – slow, heavy and menacingly distorted (Wray has stumbled on the fuzzy sound by accident, punching out a malfunctioning amp). Many radio stations ban the record because of the associations, and Dick Clark is not allowed to mention the title when introducing Wray on *American Bandstand*.

The Coasters are in a New York studio on the 17th cutting the peerless 'Three Cool Cats' and better-known 'Yakety Yak'. The latter, though not one of Leiber and Stoller's more imaginative songs, will be the group's only #1. As usual, King Curtis is on sax.

Buddy Holly and the Crickets are touring the UK, and on the 2nd make an appearance in the TV variety showcase *Sunday Night at the London Palladium*. From around this time Holly's British popularity begins to outweigh that back home.

On the 24th an era ends. In Memphis Elvis reports for military service. He is given the number 53310761.

(Above right) Eddie Cochran and (below left) Link Wray

USA

1 **Don't/I Beg of You**
Elvis Presley

2 **Get a Job**
The Silhouettes

3 **Catch a Falling Star/Magic Moments**
Perry Como

4 **Short Shorts**
The Royal Teens

5 **Twenty-Six Miles**
The Four Preps

6 **Oh, Julie**
The Crescendos

7 **Sweet Little Sixteen**
Chuck Berry

8 **Sail Along Silvery Moon /Raunchy**
Billy Vaughn

9 **At the Hop**
Danny and the Juniors

10 **It's Too Soon to Know**
Pat Boone

UK

1 **Magic Moments/Catch a Falling Star**
Perry Como

2 **The Story of My Life**
Michael Holliday

3 **Jailhouse Rock**
Elvis Presley

4 **At the Hop**
Danny and The Juniors

5 **Oh Boy**
The Crickets

6 **You are My Destiny**
Paul Anka

7 **Love Me Forever**
Marion Ryan

8 **All the Way/Chicago**
Frank Sinatra

9 **April Love**
Pat Boone

10 **Peggy Sue**
Buddy Holly

USA

1 **Tequila**
The Champs

2 **Lollipop**
The Chordettes

3 **Sweet Little Sixteen**
Chuck Berry

4 **It's Too Soon to Know**
/A Wonderful Time up There
Pat Boone

5 **Who's Sorry Now**
Connie Francis

6 **Don't/I Beg of You**
Elvis Presley

7 **Sail Along Silvery Moon**
/Raunchy
Billy Vaughn

8 **Dinner with Drac**
John Zacherle

9 **Catch a Falling Star**
/Magic Moments
Perry Como

10 **Sugartime**
The McGuire Sisters

UK

1 **Magic Moments/Catch**
a Falling Star
Perry Como

2 **Don't/I Beg of You**
Elvis Presley

3 **Whole Lotta Woman**
Marvin Rainwater

4 **Nairobi**
Tommy Steele

5 **Maybe Baby**
The Crickets

6 **La Dee Dah**
Jackie Dennis

7 **The Story of My Life**
Michael Holliday

8 **Good Golly Miss Molly**
Little Richard

9 **Swingin' Shepherd Blues**
Ted Heath

10 **Jailhouse Rock**
Elvis Presley

Chuck Willis. Inset: Carole King

On the 10th Chuck Willis dies after collapsing with a stomach ulcer, aged 30. A maker of R&B hits since early in the decade, Willis has recently crossed over into the rock'n'roll mainstream with great success, scoring heavily with 'CC Rider' in 1957 and appearing on the new Dick Clark Show. The ironically-titled 'What am I Living For?' will go gold in 1958.

A group of boys from the Bronx calling themselves Dion and the Belmonts make their recording debut for the new label Laurie with 'I Wonder Why'. It will reach #22, the first of seven Top Forty entries for the group before lead singer Dion Di Mucci's departure in 1960.

Also in New York ABC-Paramount release a first single by 16-year-old Carole King, 'The Right Girl'/'Goin'

Wild'. Neither this nor the next release will be successful, leaving King to concentrate on her writing job at Aldon Music, in the famous Brill Building. During the coming year she will meet Gerry Goffin, her future husband and co-writer of many early '60s pop classics.

Laurie London, a 13-year-old boy from London's East End, reaches #1 in the US with 'He's Got the Whole

World in His Hands'. Premièred on *6.5 Special* the previous October, the song has been a moderate hit in the UK, before, suddenly, it captures the imagination of American record-buyers. Maybe after Sputnik there's a need to reassert global control, if only in song lyrics. Despite being hopefully touted as 'the English Paul Anka', London will have no more hits.

USA

1 **Witch Doctor**
David Seville

2 **Wear My Ring around Your Neck**
Elvis Presley

3 **Twilight Time**
The Platters

4 **He's Got the Whole World in His Hands**
Laurie London

5 **Tequila**
The Champs

6 **Book of Love**
Monatones

7 **Believe What You Say /My Bucket's Got a Hole in It**
Ricky Nelson

8 **A Wonderful Time Up There /It's Too Soon to Know**
Pat Boone

9 **All I Have to Do is Dream**
The Everly Brothers

10 **Lollipop**
The Chordettes

Connie Francis looking winsome.
Inset: Lonnie Donegan

UK

1 **Whole Lotta Woman**
Marvin Rainwater

2 **It's Too Soon to Know /Wonderful Time up There**
Pat Boone

3 **Who's Sorry Now**
Connie Francis

4 **Swingin' Shepherd Blues**
Ted Heath

5 **Magic Moments /Catch a Falling Star**
Perry Como

6 **Tequila**
The Champs

6 **Grand Coolie Dam/Nobody Loves Like an Irishman**
Lonnie Donegan

8 **Lollipop**
The Chordettes

9 **Breathless**
Jerry Lee Lewis

10 **Maybe Baby**
The Crickets

At a recording session earlier in the year Connie Francis, still seeking her first solo hit, has filled out the time by recording one of her father's favourite songs from the '20s, 'Who's Sorry Now'. The plaintive song brings out the lamenting quality in her voice and the record proves a winner, eventually going to #4 in the US and #1 in Britain.

Over the next six years Francis will be the biggest-selling female pop star, with 35 Top Forty hits to her name. Possessed of not much more than an acceptable image and an evocative voice, she will, as much as anyone, typify the era. She doesn't write her own material, doesn't threaten anyone's notion of anything. She seems to be always on *American Bandstand*.

Atlantic release their fourth Bobby Darin single, and his first hit, the novelty song 'Splish Splash'. It marks the first use of their eight-track stereo recording system. Bobby Freeman's 'Do You Want to Dance', a future much-covered rock'n'roll standard, enters the charts.

On the 24th Jerry Lee Lewis begins his first UK tour and, somewhat naively, talks openly to the gutter press about his marriage to 13-year-old Myra. They proceed to crucify him. Audiences are equally hostile, booing him off the stage and Lewis cancels the tour and returns home, only to find that a nervous Sam Phillips has failed to promote 'High School Confidential'. His career as a rock'n'roll star isn't over, but it will never fully recover.

In LA three high school students – Jan Berry, Dean Torrence and Arnie Ginsburg – head for the garage with two tape recorders and two other friends, future Beach Boy Bruce Johnston and future 'Let There be Drums' star Sandy Nelson. They record a song about a local stripper that Arnie is infatuated with, 'Jennie Lee'. By the time Arwin Records has decided to put it out Dean has been called up, and the record is credited to Jan and Arnie. It reaches #8.

One new entry is Jerry Butler and the Impressions' 'For Your Precious Love', co-written by Butler and Impression Curtis Mayfield. Butler will split from the group later in the year, but he and Mayfield will carry on writing together, producing hits for Butler into the next decade. Mayfield himself will guide the Impressions to huge success as one of the most original and influential black groups of the '60s, before launching his own solo career.

On the 11th Cochran's 'Summertime Blues' is released. In New York Buddy Holly records without the Crickets for the first time. While visiting a music publisher he meets Maria Elena Santiago, whom he will marry in Lubbock on 15 August.

In Britain a pilot for the forthcoming TV show *Oh Boy* goes out. Top of the bill is Marty Wilde, who has just recorded a version of Jody Reynolds's death-disc 'Endless Sleep'. It will be the first of four consecutive top five hits, all of them cover versions.

USA

1 **All I Have to Do is Dream /Claudette**
Everly Brothers

2 **Witch Doctor**
David Seville

3 **Wear My Ring around Your Neck**
Elvis Presley

4 **Twilight Time**
The Platters

5 **Looking Back/Do I Like It?**
Nat 'King' Cole

6 **Big Man**
Four Preps

7 **Purple People Eater**
Sheb Wooley

8 **Secretly/Make Me a Miracle**
Jimmie Rodgers

9 **He's Got the Whole World in His Hands**
Laurie London

10 **Do You Want to Dance?**
Bobby Freeman

UK

1 **Who's Sorry Now**
Connie Francis

2 **It's Too Soon to Know /Wonderful Time up There**
Pat Boone

3 **Tom Hark**
Elias and his Zig Zag Jive Flutes

4 **Wear My Ring around Your Neck**
Elvis Presley

5 **Grand Coolie Dam/Nobody Loves Like an Irishman**
Lonnie Donegan

6 **Lollipop**
The Mudlarks

7 **Stairway of Love**
Michael Holliday

8 **Witch Doctor**
Don Lang

9 **All I Have to Do is Dream /Claudette**
The Everly Brothers

10 **Tulips from Amsterdam /Hands**
Max Bygraves

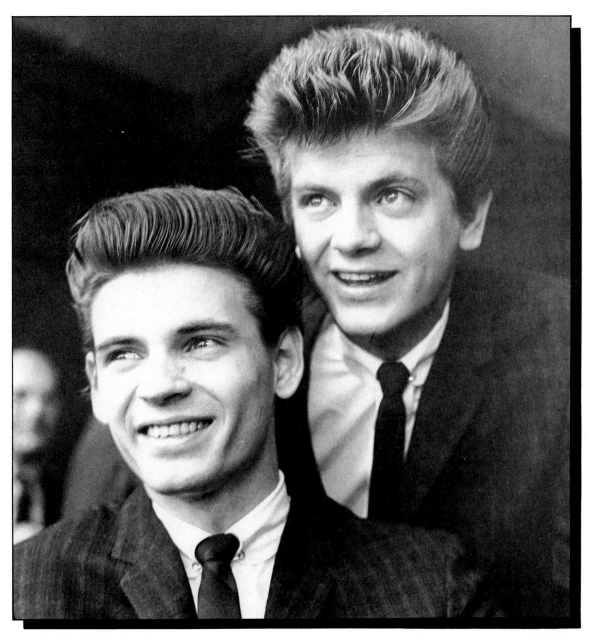

The Everly Brothers.

USA

1 **Purple People Eater**
Sheb Wooley

2 **Yakety Yak**
The Coasters

3 **All I Have to Do is Dream /Claudette**
The Everly Brothers

4 **Witch Doctor**
David Seville

5 **Secretly/Make Me a Miracle**
Jimmie Rodgers

6 **Endless Sleep**
Jody Reynolds

7 **Return to Me**
Dean Martin

8 **Jennie Lee**
Jan and Arnie

9 **Do You Want to Dance?**
Bobby Freeman

10 **Big Man**
The Four Preps

UK

1 **All I Have to Do is Dream /Claudette**
The Everly Brothers

2 **On the Street Where You Live**
Vic Damone

3 **Tulips from Amsterdam /Hands**
Max Bygraves

4 **Big Man**
The Four Preps

5 **Who's Sorry Now**
Connie Francis

6 **Book of Love**
The Mudlarks

7 **The Army Game**
TV Cast

8 **Witch Doctor**
Don Lang

9 **Stairway of Love**
Michael Holliday

10 **Tom Hark**
Elias and his Zig Zag Jive Flutes

Duane Eddy

Perhaps it's the hot summer, but there's something of a backlash against rock'n'roll. On Capitol Hill a counsel for the American Guild of Authors and Composers plays 'Yakety Yak' to a Senate Committee on the industry, claiming it cheapens American music. A Catholic magazine in Minneapolis launches a national competition in wholesome lyric-writing, and mentions Elvis Presley's 'Wear Your Ring around My Neck' as an example of the opposite. The Exxon Gas Research Center reports that drivers who listen to rock'n'roll in their cars may be unconsciously wasting gas by keeping time on the accelerator pedal.

Meanwhile the creative process continues. In Los Angeles 18-year-old Phil Spector and two friends record a song written around the inscription on his father's tombstone – 'To Know Him is to Love Him'. They will release it in August under the name of the Teddy Bears.

Duane Eddy enters the Top Forty for the first time with 'Rebel Rouser'. Like the first single 'Movin'n'groovin'', it has been produced by Lee Hazlewood, financed by him and Los Angeles music entrepreneur Lester Sill. The distinctive 'twangy' sound of Eddy's guitar has been achieved by playing the melody on the bottom strings, then feeding it through an echo chamber which Hazlewood has created out of a grain storage elevator at his Phoenix studio. Once a strong rhythm section, manic shouts and some insistent sax have been added, the effect is of loose energy on the prowl.

The Everly Brothers are nearing the end of an eight-week run at the top of the British chart. After the failure of their third single, a version of Ray Charles's 'This Little Girl of Mine', they've gone back to the Bryants, authors of 'Bye Bye Love', for the fourth. Reportedly written by Boudleaux Bryant in 15 minutes, 'All I Have to Do is Dream' has broken with the uptempo style of their first two hits, and allowed full rein to the boys' beautiful harmony singing. Over the next few years they will enjoy a virtually unbroken string of hits, nearly all written by the Bryants or themselves.

The flip of 'Dream' is one of the rare exceptions. Having run into Roy Orbison at a concert in Gary, Indiana, the brothers ask him if he has any new songs. He plays them one he has just written about his wife Claudette, they like it, and he scribbles it down for them on a cardboard box. Now, with 'Claudette' a success in its own right – making #30 in the US, #6 in the UK – Orbison has been given the boost he needs to abandon Sun, move to Nashville, and concentrate on his writing.

On the 23rd, as if to further emphasize the brothers' influence, the Kalin Twins succeed them at the top of the British charts with 'When', a record that sounds more like the Everlys than the Everlys do.

In the US the month begins with Ricky Nelson at #1 for the first time with 'Poor Little Fool', a record which somehow manages to bounce with self-pity. But by mid-month it's the Everly Brothers again, this time with 'Bird Dog'.

USA

1 **Hard-Headed Woman /Don't Ask Me Why**
Elvis Presley

2 **Patricia**
Perez Prado

3 **Poor Little Fool**
Ricky Nelson

4 **Splish Splash**
Bobby Darin

5 **Yakety Yak**
The Coasters

6 **Rebel-'Rouser**
Duane Eddy

7 **When**
Kalin Twins

8 **Purple People Eater**
Sheb Wooley

9 **My True Love/Leroy**
Jack Scott

10 **Endless Sleep**
Jody Reynolds

UK

1 **All I Have to Do is Dream /Claudette**
The Everly Brothers

2 **Hard Headed Woman**
Elvis Presley

3 **Big Man**
The Four Preps

4 **Rave On**
Buddy Holly

5 **When**
The Kalin Twins

6 **Tulips from Amsterdam /Hands**
Max Bygraves

7 **Endless Sleep**
Marty Wilde

8 **Twilight Time**
The Platters

9 **On the Street Where You Live**
Vic Damone

10 **Return to Me**
Dean Martin

It's what you do with your hands – the Everly Brothers and (inset) the Kalin Twins

The British TV show *Oh Boy* starts its regular run on the 13th. Marty Wilde again tops the bill, but the show, and British pop for the next few decades, belongs to someone else. Cliff Richard, a young North Londoner with a passion for Elvis, has been playing with the Drifters for several months. A demo and word-of-mouth recommendation have won them an EMI contract, and the first single, 'Schoolboy Crush'/'Move It', has been released on 29 August.

For the *Oh Boy* debut producer Jack Good advises Cliff to flip the single, cut the sideburns, perform without his guitar, and generally not to worry about repressing his sexuality. He's a sensation,

and 'Move It' begins climbing the charts.

A tour is arranged, but the band are a guitarist short. Manager John Foster runs into Hank B. Marvin while looking for someone else. Marvin agrees to join up if his friend Bruce Welch can also be accommodated. Half the classic Drifters (soon to be renamed the Shadows) line-up is now in place.

In the States Connie Francis has her second Top Twenty hit with the bouncy 'Stupid Cupid'. It's written by 19-year-old Neil Sedaka, who'll soon be churning out hits with lyricist Howie Greenfield. New entries on the US chart include the Isley Brothers' 'Shout', Big Bopper's only Top Ten hit, 'Chantilly Lace', and

the doo-wop classic Harvey and the Moonglows' 'Ten Commandments of Love'.

USA

1 **Volare**
Domenico Modugno
2 **Little Star**
Elegants
3 **Bird Dog/Devoted to You**
Everly Brothers
4 **Just a Dream**
Jimmy Clanton
5 **Poor Little Fool**
Ricky Nelson
6 **Patricia**
Perez Prado
7 **My True Love/Leroy**
Jack Scott
8 **Splish Splash**
Bobby Darin
9 **When**
Kalin Twins
10 **Are You Really Mine?
/The Wizard**
Jimmie Rodgers

UK

1 **When**
The Kalin Twins
2 **All I Have to Do is Dream**
The Everly Brothers
3 **Return to Me**
Dean Martin
4 **Endless Sleep**
Marty Wilde
5 **Hard Headed Woman**
Elvis Presley
6 **Carolina Moon/Stupid Cupid**
Connie Francis
7 **Tulips from Amsterdam
/Hands**
Max Bygraves
8 **Rave On**
Buddy Holly
9 **Patricia**
Perez Prado
10 **Yakety Yak**
The Coasters

Marty, Cliff and assorted co-stars on 'Oh Boy!'

On the 6th, *Billboard* publishes an article warning that payola – in essence, record companies slipping under-the-turntable payments to disc jockeys in return for airplay – is becoming 'a monster that may yet destroy its creators'. No names are mentioned. Yet.

Buddy Holly is now living in New York, married to Maria Elena and divorced from the Crickets. Over the last 18 months, at various sessions in New Mexico, he has recorded most of the songs for which he will be best remembered – including 'Peggy Sue', 'Listen to Me', 'Everyday', 'Words of Love', 'Rave On', 'Heartbeat' and 'Wishing'. In New York on the 21st he has his last studio recording session, putting down four songs – 'It Doesn't Matter Anymore', 'True Love Ways', 'Moondreams' and 'Raining in My Heart' – with string accompaniment from the Dick Jacobs Orchestra.

Conway Twitty's 'It's Only Make Believe' enters the US chart, on its way to #1. In most respects the record closely resembles any number of dramatic ballads from the pre-rock'n'roll era, but in the instrumentation used and the rampant emotionalism of the performance – which seems aimed so far over the top as to approach self-parody – it is very much a product of the rock'n'roll age.

James Brown and the Famous Flames' 'Try Me', released by Federal, will be their first pop chart entry and first R&B #1.

In Liverpool young tugboat sailor Ronald Wycherly turns up backstage at a Marty Wilde concert with some songs to sell. After he's played and sung one of them,

promoter Larry Parnes signs him up for the rest of the tour and gives him a new name – Billy Fury.

'Now this is just supposition . . .' Conway Twitty in defensive posture

USA

1 **It's All in the Game**
Tommy Edwards

2 **Volare**
Domenico Modugno

3 **Bird Dog/Devoted to You**
The Everly Brothers

4 **Rock-in' Robin/Over and Over**
Bobby Day

5 **Little Star**
The Elegants

6 **Patricia**
Perez Prado

7 **Tears on My Pillow**
Little Anthony and
The Imperials

8 **Susie Darlin'**
Robin Luke

9 **Tea for Two Cha-Cha**
Tommy Dorsey Orchestra

10 **Just a Dream**
Jimmy Clanton

UK

1 **Stupid Cupid/Carolina Moon**
Connie Francis

2 **When**
The Kalin Twins

3 **Volare**
Dean Martin

4 **Bird Dog**
The Everly Brothers

5 **Return to Me**
Dean Martin

6 **Mad Passionate Love**
Bernard Bresslaw

7 **Poor Little Fool**
Ricky Nelson

8 **Splish Splash/Hello My Darlings**
Charlie Drake

9 **Endless Sleep**
Marty Wilde

10 **Fever**
Peggy Lee

The Kingston Trio are at #1 with 'Tom Dooley', a cheery folk tune about a murderer. Even more significantly the album from which it is taken squeezes between Sinatra and Mitch Miller to top the album chart for a week.

The tunes may be mostly traditional, played on mostly traditional instruments, but it's a contemporary sound and a contemporary sensibility the Kingston Trio are selling, a music fit to accompany the looming end of the Eisenhower era and the dawn of Kennedy's America. Their success over the next two years will be phenomenal, and in its wake will come other groups like the Limeliters, the Chad Mitchell Trio, the New Christy Minstrels and the Highwaymen. From these groups will spring the founding fathers of electrified folk – musicians such as Gene Clark and Jim McGuinn.

At the other end of the musical spectrum R&B group Hank Ballard and the Midnighters, who've had only minor success since the 'Annie' hits of 1954–5, record 'Teardrops on Your Letter' in Cincinnati. This will make the charts, but later be more famous for its 'B' side, the original version of 'The Twist'.

On the 10th Sam Cooke suffers only minor injuries in a road accident near Marion, Arkansas. Also injured is Lou Rawls, lead singer of the Pilgrim Travelers Quartet, who will later share the vocals on Cooke's classic 'Bring It on Home to Me'.

Cliff Richard's 'Move It', released in the US, sinks without trace.

USA

1 **It's All in the Game**
Tommy Edwards

2 **It's Only Make Believe**
Conway Twitty

3 **Topsy II**
Cozy Cole

4 **Tom Dooley**
Kingston Trio

5 **Rock-in' Robin**
Bobby Day

6 **Chantilly Lace**
Big Bopper

7 **Tea for Two Cha-Cha**
Tommy Dorsey Orchestra

8 **The End**
Earl Grant

9 **Tears on My Pillow**
Little Anthony & The Imperials

10 **Bird Dog/Devoted to You**
The Everly Brothers

UK

1 **Stupid Cupid/Carolina Moon**
Connie Francis

2 **King Creole**
Elvis Presley

3 **Move It**
Cliff Richard

4 **Bird Dog**
The Everly Brothers

5 **A Certain Smile**
Johnny Mathis

6 **Come Prima/Volare**
Marino Marini

7 **Born Too Late**
The Poni-Tails

8 **Volare**
Dean Martin

9 **It's All in the Game**
Tommy Edwards

10 **More Than Ever**
Malcolm Vaughan

Horn-rimmed sincerity – the Kingston Trio

The Teddy Bears' 'To Know Him is to Love Him' holds the US #1 spot for three weeks, but the album they put together doesn't fare so well. Imperial expects 12 tracks to be recorded in a six-hour session, but Spector, working at what even to him seems like breakneck pace, can only manage three. The rest of the album has to be padded out with hurriedly recorded versions of standards, and Spector has been given a useful lesson in how not to make records.

Ritchie Valens enters the Top Forty with a double-sided hit. The classic teen ballad 'Donna' will reach #2, the even more durable Mexican rocker 'La Bamba' #22. The Platters' 'Smoke Gets in Your Eyes' is on its way to the top, their fourth US #1 in three years. Jackie Wilson makes #1 in the R&B chart and has his first Top Ten pop chart entry with another song part-written by Berry Gordy Jr, 'Lonely Teardrops'. Neil Sedaka signs up with RCA as a performer.

Saving a few honourable exceptions, the aggression seems to have drained out of rock'n'roll over the year. It ends with 'The Chipmunk Song' at #1 in the US, Conway Twitty #1 in the UK, and Mitch Miller atop the album chart. Three of the founding fathers – Elvis Presley, Jerry Lee Lewis and Little Richard – have been removed, one way or another, from the main stage. Only Chuck Berry remains, and his luck will run out in 1959.

The Teddy Bears, with Phil Spector on the right

USA

1 **To Know Him is to Love Him**
Teddy Bears

2 **Tom Dooley**
Kingston Trio

3 **It's Only Make Believe**
Conway Twitty

4 **Beep Beep**
The Playmates

5 **One Night**
Elvis Presley

6 **Topsy II**
Cozy Cole

7 **Lonesome Town**
Ricky Nelson

8 **Problems**
The Everly Brothers

9 **I Got Stung**
Elvis Presley

10 **It's All in the Game**
Tommy Edwards

UK

1 **Hoots Mon**
Lord Rockingham's XI

2 **It's Only Make Believe**
Conway Twitty

3 **It's All in the Game**
Tommy Edwards

4 **Tom Dooley**
Lonnie Donegan

5 **Bird Dog**
The Everly Brothers

6 **A Certain Smile**
Johnny Mathis

7 **More Than Ever**
Malcolm Vaughan

8 **Come Prima/Volare**
Marino Marini

9 **Come On Let's Go**
Tommy Steele

10 **High Class Baby**
Cliff Richard

1959

According to Don McLean's 'American Pie' this was the year the music died, but things weren't quite that simple. True, Buddy Holly's death, the payola scandal and Chuck Berry's removal from the scene seemed to mark the end of more than just the decade. True, it was the year the music looked at its most artificial, with a series of cut-out teen heroes like Fabian and Frankie Avalon singing processed songs on processed TV shows. But it was also the year in which echoey post-rock'n'roll pop reached a glorious apotheosis with immaculately crafted records like Bobby Darin's 'Dream Lover', Neil Sedaka's 'Oh! Carol' and Paul Anka's 'Lonely Boy'.

And there were new beginnings to match the endings. The British were starting to catch up, creating their own roster of stars and laying the groundwork for the '60s group explosion. In America there was a minor first hit for the Miracles, enormous album success for the Kingston Trio and Leiber and Stoller's ground-breaking work with the Drifters – three early hints of the shape of the decade to come.

Connie Francis

Lloyd Price's 'Stagger Lee' enters the US Top Forty on the 5th; it will be #1 for most of February. Stagger Lee himself is a legendary black gambler-killer from turn-of-the-century times who has been immortalized in more songs (or more variations of the same song) than anyone can remember. Price, who has a string of R&B hits to his name (including the original 'Lawdy Miss Clawdy' back in 1952), wails the old story to a hard rock accompaniment.

Or tries to. When the time comes for him to sing the song on *American Bandstand* a problem arises – Dick Clark has realized that the lyrics seem to celebrate gambling and murder, and in uncertain racial circumstances at that. The lyrics have to be changed, and not only for the TV show – a whole new version is recorded and put out in place of the original.

Buddy Holly agrees to headline a tour of the Mid-West with Dion and the Belmonts, the Big Bopper and Ritchie Valens. In the days before departure he makes his last recordings, accompanying himself on guitar in the New York apartment. Norman Petty will supervise the overdubbing of these songs – which include 'Peggy Sue Got Married', 'Crying, Wishing and Hoping' and 'Learning the Game' – after Holly's death.

Ricky Nelson makes his big screen dramatic debut alongside John Wayne and Dean Martin in Howard Hawks's *Rio Bravo*, playing young guitar-playing gunslinger Colorado. The 'flowerpot through the window' scene, in which Ricky and Angie Dickinson combine to rescue John Wayne from trouble, soon attains cult status among Western connoisseurs.

USA

1 **The Chipmunk Song**
David Seville
& The Chipmunks

2 **Smoke Gets in Your Eyes**
The Platters

3 **To Know Him is to Love Him**
Teddy Bears

4 **One Night**
Elvis Presley

5 **Problems**
The Everly Brothers

6 **Tom Dooley**
Kingston Trio

7 **Lonesome Town**
Ricky Nelson

8 **Beep Beep**
The Playmates

9 **A Lover's Question**
Clyde McPhatter

10 **Whole Lotta Lovin'**
Fats Domino

UK

1 **It's Only Make Believe**
Conway Twitty

2 **Hoots Mon**
Lord Rockingham's XI

3 **Tom Dooley**
Lonnie Donegan

4 **Tom Dooley**
The Kingston Trio

5 **Love Makes The World Go Round**
Perry Como

6 **Tea for Two Cha-Cha**
Tommy Dorsey Orchestra

7 **It's All in the Game**
Tommy Edwards

8 **High Class Baby**
Cliff Richard

9 **The Day the Rains Came**
Jane Morgan

10 **More Party Pops**
Russ Conway

Lloyd Price. Inset: Dion (centre) and the Belmonts

February 1959

On the 2nd the 'Winter Dance Party' tour plays Clear Lake, Iowa. After the evening concert Buddy Holly, unwilling to face the prospect of another 400-mile trip in a freezing bus, decides to journey on to the next gig in Moorhead, Minnesota, by plane. According to legend the Big Bopper hitches a ride from him, and Ritchie Valens wins the last seat on the toss of a coin from Holly back-up man and future country star Waylon Jennings. In the early hours of the 3rd, not long after take-off from Mason City, the light plane crashes in a heavy blizzard, killing all on board.

Later in the month the ironically titled 'It Doesn't Matter Anymore' enters both the US and UK charts, rising to #1 in the latter.

USA

1 **Smoke Gets in Your Eyes**
The Platters

2 **All American Boy**
Bill Parsons

3 **Donna**
Ritchie Valens

4 **Sixteen Candles**
The Crests

5 **Stagger Lee**
Lloyd Price

6 **My Happiness**
Connie Francis

7 **Gotta Travel On**
Billy Grammar

8 **Lonely Teardrops**
Jackie Wilson

9 **A Lover's Question**
Clyde McPhatter

10 **Goodbye Baby**
Jack Scott

UK

1 **I Got Stung/One Night**
Elvis Presley

2 **Baby Face**
Little Richard

3 **To Know Him is to Love Him**
The Teddy Bears

4 **Kiss Me Honey**
Shirley Bassey

5 **Problems**
The Everly Brothers

6 **As I Love You**
Shirley Bassey

7 **Smoke Gets in Your Eyes**
The Platters

8 **The Day the Rains Came**
Jane Morgan

9 **It's Only Make Believe**
Conway Twitty

10 **High School Confidential**
Jerry Lee Lewis

One man's plane crash is another's biggest break. On the 3rd the local radio station for Fargo and Moorhead broadcasts an appeal for acts to fill the gaps tragedy has left in that evening's concert. Robert Veeline (soon to be Bobby Vee) offers himself and his group, the Shadows. They play second on the programme, and do well enough to impress a local promoter. He will arrange more gigs for them, and eventually help them secure a recording contract.

With rather less publicity than the Iowa threesome, Eddie 'Guitar Slim' Jones dies in New York, aged 33, of pneumonia. His best known song is 'The Things That I Used to Do'. Jimi Hendrix will later cite Jones's extravagant electric guitar style as one of the major influences on him.

Buddy Holly. Inset: Bobby Vee practising the Frank Sinatra stool-style

The Drifters, who have not enjoyed much success since the defection of Clyde McPhatter in 1956, have a new lead singer, Ben E. King. They have also just completed a recording session considered a disaster by all concerned, including producers Leiber and Stoller. But as the pair dredge the tapes for anything salvageable, one song proves impossible to ignore. Though it's out of tune, sounds like two songs at once, and is in fact a complete mess, the overall effect still manages to be utterly compelling. It simply has to be released.

'There Goes My Baby', with its strange mix of Latin rhythms, gospel vocals and stark sweeping strings, not only goes to #2 on the pop chart, but also shatters the conventional limitations surrounding black group music, and helps to open the way for Phil Spector and other innovators of the 60s.

More conventionally, Frankie Avalon is at #1 with 'Venus', and Fabian has just been voted 'most promising new singer' by *American Bandstand* viewers. Ricky Nelson has another double-sided chart entry: 'It's Late' is a re-working of the 'Wake up Little Susie' theme with wittier lyrics and wonderful piled rhymes, and 'Never be Anyone Else But You' is a romantic ballad of seductive simplicity. Both sides will make the Top Ten.

Another double-sider will do even better. Elvis Presley's 'A Fool Such as I'/'I Need Your Love Tonight' goes gold on release, eventually reaching #2 and #4 on the US chart. The gold record is shipped out to Germany, presumably for Elvis to keep under his bunk.

EMI announces it is discontinuing the sale of 78s. Kids stop buying them, investors start.

USA

1. **Stagger Lee**
   Lloyd Price
2. **Donna**
   Ritchie Valens
3. **Charlie Brown**
   The Coasters
4. **Sixteen Candles**
   Crests
5. **Petite Fleur**
   Chris Barber
6. **I Cried a Tear**
   LaVern Baker
7. **Venus**
   Frankie Avalon
8. **Peter Gunn Theme**
   Ray Anthony
9. **All American Boy**
   Bill Parsons
10. **Alvin's Harmonica**
    David Seville
    & The Chipmunks

UK

1. **Smoke Gets in Your Eyes**
   The Platters
2. **As I Love You**
   Shirley Bassey
3. **Does Your Chewing Gum Lose its Flavour**
   Lonnie Donegan
4. **I Got Stung/One Night**
   Elvis Presley
5. **Pub with No Beer**
   Slim Dusty
6. **Side Saddle**
   Russ Conway
7. **My Happiness**
   Connie Francis
8. **Petite Fleur**
   Chris Barber
9. **Little Drummer Boy**
   The Beverley Sisters
10. **To Know Him is to Love Him**
    The Teddy Bears

The Drifters, with lead singer Ben E. King (left)

Bobby Darin's 'Dream Lover', one of the great pop classics of the late '50s, is released. Darin has written it himself, determined to prove that he too can wring the ultimate pop song out of C, Am, F and G7. Overlapping male and female choruses swim out of a supernatural ether, the melody rolls in on a chunky rhythm, a pizzicato string effect provides an eerie counterpoint to Darin's yearning voice. It's just a simple love song and it sounds like it comes from another world. It goes to #2 in the US and #1 in the UK.

Another, albeit less transcendental classic enters the charts. 'A Teenager in Love' will be the only Dion and the Belmonts million-seller, reaching #5 in the US but only the lower reaches of the Top Thirty in the UK, where there are two cover versions. Marty Wilde's is the more successful, and Craig Douglas, one of the growing breed of British pop stars owing more to Pat Boone than Elvis Presley, abandons the contest and rushes out a cover of Sam Cooke's 'Only Sixteen'. This will take him to #1, and usher in two years of

continuing Top Twenty successes.

More original than either Wilde or Douglas, Billy Fury reaches the Top Twenty with his first single, the self-penned 'Maybe Tomorrow'. His success owes something to both national tour exposure and, particularly, appearances on *Oh Boy*. British success is now heavily dependent on the TV shows; a new one, *Drumbeat*, begins on the 4th. It will only last until August, but in the meantime will go a long way toward making a star of another new singer, Adam Faith.

USA

1 **Venus**
Frankie Avalon

2 **Come Softly to Me**
The Fleetwoods

3 **Charlie Brown**
The Coasters

4 **It's Just a Matter of Time**
Brook Benton

5 **Tragedy**
Thomas Wayne

6 **Alvin's Harmonica**
David Seville
        & The Chipmunks

7 **Never Be Anyone Else But You**
Ricky Nelson

8 **Pink Shoelaces**
Dodie Stevens

9 **I've Had It**
Bell Notes

10 **It's Late**
Ricky Nelson

UK

1 **Side Saddle**
Russ Conway

2 **Smoke Gets in Your Eyes**
The Platters

3 **It Doesn't Matter Any More**
Buddy Holly

4 **My Happiness**
Connie Francis

5 **As I Love You**
Shirley Bassey

6 **Petite Fleur**
Chris Barber

7 **Stagger Lee**
Lloyd Price

8 **Pub with No Beer**
Slim Dusty

9 **Little Drummer Boy**
The Beverley Sisters

10 **Gigi**
Billy Eckstine

Bobby Darin

USA

1 **Come Softly to Me**
The Fleetwoods

2 **A Fool Such As I**
Elvis Presley

3 **Venus**
Frankie Avalon

4 **Pink Shoelaces**
Dodie Stevens

5 **Guitar Boogie Shuffle**
The Virtues

6 **The Happy Organ**
Dave (Baby) Cortez

7 **I Need Your Love Tonight**
Elvis Presley

8 **Tell Him No**
Travis and Bob

9 **Sorry, I Ran All the Way Home**
The Impalas

10 **Turn Me Loose**
Fabian

UK

1 **A Fool Such As I/I Need Your Love Tonight**
Elvis Presley

2 **It Doesn't Matter Anymore**
Buddy Holly

3 **Side Saddle**
Russ Conway

4 **Donna**
Marty Wilde

5 **Petite Fleur**
Chris Barber

6 **It's Late/Never be Anyone Else But You**
Ricky Nelson

7 **Charlie Brown**
The Coasters

8 **C'mon Everybody**
Eddie Cochran

9 **Smoke Gets in your Eyes**
The Platters

10 **Come Softly to Me**
The Fleetwoods

The month begins with Buddy Holly at #1 in the UK with 'It Doesn't Matter Any More'. The fact that the record has only reached #13 in the US will, in retrospect, prove no accident. Holly's legacy as one of the pioneer singer-songwriter-guitarists – stressing melody, a willingness to experiment, the acceptability of a vulnerable male image – will be better absorbed in Britain, and will play an important role in the group explosion of the '60s.

The first American #1 of the month is a sublimely titled instrumental, 'The Happy Organ' by Dave 'Baby' Cortez. Wilbert Harrison's dynamic version of Leiber and Stoller's 'Kansas City' takes over for a fortnight, before Johnny Horton begins a six-week run with his 'The Battle of New Orleans'. This is the first of three songs built around historical events – 'North to Alaska' and 'Sink the Bismarck' are the others – which Horton will take into the top four. The sound is almost pure country, but the subject-matter is sufficiently non-traditional to break down genre boundaries.

In Britain Neil Sedaka has his first chart entry with 'I Go Ape', and Cliff Richard's first movie, *Serious Charge*, is premièred in London. To no one's great surprise Cliff plays a semi-delinquent trying to make it as a rock singer. On the 30th the last *Oh Boy* for twenty years goes out on ITV.

On the 29th in Herndon Stadium, Atlanta, one of the first outdoor rock festivals takes place, with Ray Charles, B. B. King and the Drifters performing. It rains.

Johnny Horton – the singer as history teacher

65

The first *Juke Box Jury* television programme goes out on the BBC. A panel of four, at least some of whom know something about music, listens to new releases played by host David Jacobs. They comment on what a good beat a record has (or hasn't), make a few bad jokes, and pronounce the record a hit or miss. Occasionally the artists concerned, hidden from the panel but not the viewers by a screen, have to listen to how untalented they are. The show is a great success and is to run, in the same format, for years in the same slot on early Saturday evenings.

Presumably some young Brits are holding their tape recorders close to the screen. *Billboard* sends shivers down the industry's backbone by claiming that American teenagers are taping music from the radio in order to avoid the cost of buying records.

Eddie Cochran cuts 'Somethin' Else', the third and weakest of his three teen anthems. It fails to reach the US Top Forty, but climbs to #22 in Britain, where Cochran has attracted a more loyal following. US Top One Hundred entries include Sam Cooke's 'Only Sixteen' and Chuck Berry's 'Back in the USA'. In Britain Duane Eddy's 'Peter Gunn' and Lloyd Price's 'Personality' enter the Top Twenty.

On the 5th Bob Zimmerman graduates from Hibbing High School. In the coming summer he will get a couple of nights' work playing piano for Bobby Vee and the Shadows, before the band decide they'd rather have someone who can play in more than one key.

USA

1 **The Battle of New Orleans**
Johnny Horton

2 **Kansas City**
Wilbert Harrison

3 **Dream Lover**
Bobby Darin

4 **Quiet Village**
Martin Denny

5 **Personality**
Lloyd Price

6 **A Teenager in Love**
Dion & The Belmonts

7 **Kookie, Kookie (Lend Me Your Comb)**
Ed Byrnes with Connie Stevens

8 **Sorry, I Ran All the Way Home**
The Impalas

9 **Only You**
Frank Pourcel

10 **The Happy Organ**
Dave (Baby) Cortez

UK

1 **A Fool Such As I/I Need Your Love Tonight**
Elvis Presley

2 **It Doesn't Matter Anymore**
Buddy Holly

3 **Roulette**
Russ Conway

4 **It's Late/Never be Anyone Else But You**
Ricky Nelson

5 **I've Waited So Long**
Anthony Newley

6 **Guitar Boogie Shuffle**
Bert Weedon

7 **Donna**
Marty Wilde

8 **Side Saddle**
Russ Conway

9 **Mean Streak/Never Mind**
Cliff Richard

10 **I Go Ape**
Neil Sedaka

'They're really rockin' on bandstands ...'

Paul Anka is at #1 with another anthem for affluent American male youth. A drum roll leads the way into 'Lonely Boy', igniting a rolling rhythm and one of those heavenly strings and voices backdrops in which it's hard to tell which is which. Out front young Paul doesn't so much feel sorry for himself as positively reverberate with self-pity. It rivals 'It's Only Make Believe' as the most over-the-top song of the age.

Ray Charles enters the charts with the classic 'What'd I Say', and the Shirelles make their chart debut, reaching #83 with 'Dedicated to the One I Love'. It will do rather better when re-released in 1961, reaching #3, and the Mamas and the Papas will go one notch higher with the song in 1967.

On the 16th the Coasters record Leiber and Stoller's 'Poison Ivy' and 'What About Us?' in New York. The former, though not one of Leiber and Stoller's finest, will reach #7, and in any case deserves immortality for the rhyme 'you're gonna need an ocean/of calamine lotion'. The latter, released as a 'B' side the following year, will contain a more menacing message for Americans in the '60s – 'he's gotta car made of suede . . . if we go out on dates we go on a box on roller skates'.

Two women of great importance to American music make the news, one starting out, the other saying goodbye. On the 11th Joan Baez records for the first time – a duet with Bob Gibson at the Newport Folk Festival – and six days later Billie Holliday dies, aged 44, in a New York hospital. She has just been arrested on her death-bed for heroin possession.

USA

1 **The Battle of New Orleans**
Johnny Horton

2 **Personality**
Lloyd Price

3 **Lonely Boy**
Paul Anka

4 **Dream Lover**
Bobby Darin

5 **Lipstick on Your Collar**
Connie Francis

6 **Tallahassee Lassie**
Freddy Cannon

7 **Kansas City**
Wilbert Harrison

8 **Quiet Village**
Martin Denny

9 **Along Came Jones**
Coasters

10 **A Teenager in Love**
Dion & The Belmonts

UK

1 **Dream Lover**
Bobby Darin

2 **Roulette**
Russ Conway

3 **A Teenager in Love**
Marty Wilde

4 **Battle of New Orleans**
Lonnie Donegan

5 **A Fool Such as I/I Need Your Love Tonight**
Elvis Presley

6 **Personality**
Anthony Newley

7 **I've Waited So Long**
Anthony Newley

8 **Peter Gunn**
Duane Eddy

9 **Side Saddle**
Russ Conway

10 **Personality**
Lloyd Price

The Shirelles

Since 'Only You' in 1955 the Platters have had 14 further entries in the US Top Forty, including three other number ones. On the evening of the 10th, police burst into a room in Cincinnati's Sheraton Gibston Hotel, where the group have just finished a three-day engagement. The four male members of the quintet are entertaining four young women, three of them white. Certain items of clothing have been removed.

The four Platters are charged with aiding and abetting prostitution,

tawdry indulgence in lust'. His remarks, and the business as a whole, seem to many to reek of racism. Despite their acquittal the Platters' career will never recover its former glory.

Nor will Bobby Darin's, if for totally different reasons. Having, in 'Dream Lover', written the perfect pop song, Darin proceeds to abandon the field, recording and releasing the Brecht-Weill song from *The Threepenny Opera*, 'Mack the Knife'. It will be both his and the year's biggest hit, spending nine weeks at #1. For the next

USA

1 **Lonely Boy**
Paul Anka

2 **A Big Hunk o' Love**
Elvis Presley

3 **My Heart is an Open Book**
Carl Dobkins Jr.

4 **The Battle of New Orleans**
Johnny Horton

5 **Tiger**
Fabian

6 **There Goes My Baby**
The Drifters

7 **Waterloo**
Stonewall Jackson

8 **Lavender Blue**
Sammy Turner

9 **Sweeter Than You**
Ricky Nelson

10 **Forty Miles of Bad Road**
Duane Eddy

UK

1 **Living Doll**
Cliff Richard

2 **Dream Lover**
Bobby Darin

3 **Battle of New Orleans**
Lonnie Donegan

4 **Big Hunk o' Love**
Elvis Presley

5 **A Teenager in Love**
Marty Wilde

6 **Lipstick on Your Collar**
Connie Francis

7 **Roulette**
Russ Conway

8 **Peter Gunn**
Duane Eddy

9 **Heart of a Man**
Frankie Vaughan

10 **Personality**
Anthony Newley

lewdness and assignation. In December they will be acquitted on all charges, a detail which does nothing to stop the judge accusing them of a 'socially abhorrent,

couple of years Darin will concentrate on recording standards and making films.

European songs are all the rage. The US #1 at the end of the month is the Browns' 'The

Three Bells', a story of small-town religious sanctity which sounds as American as apple pie. In fact it's a 15-year-old French song made famous by Edith Piaf.

The Platters – before the bust

Boy Meets Girl starts up on British TV as a replacement for *Oh Boy*, with the same resident star, Marty Wilde. His latest single, a cover of Phil Phillips's 'Sea of Love' (#2 in the US), enters the UK charts. The record has all the conviction that can be expected from someone who has just announced that he wants to give up rock'n'roll and 'do real class ballad stuff like Sinatra'.

Cliff Richard's 'Living Doll', which has just finished a three-week run at #1, may not be rock'n'roll but at least it's no nearer Sinatra. He's now Britain's top star.

Bobby Vee and the Shadows enter the US charts with their first record, Vee's own composition 'Suzy Baby'. It reaches #77. Drum-sound, guitar-sound and vocal-sound are all pure Buddy Holly. There are worse models to build a career on.

Two instrumentals also make entries, headed for #5 and #4 respectively. Johnny and the Hurricanes' 'Red River Rock', adapted from the traditional 'Red River Valley', is the group's second hit, but the first to use their musical signature: Paul Tesluk's electric organ as lead instrument. Sandy Nelson, drummer on both Jan and Dean's 'Jennie Lee' and the Teddy Bears' 'To Know Him is to Love Him', brings an even

simpler gimmick to 'Teen Beat' – the drums are pushed out in front of everything else.

On the 7th Dick Clark's stage show at Michigan State Fair breaks all attendance records, with 15,000 turning up to see the likes of the Coasters, Duane Eddy, Jan and Dean, Frankie Avalon, Bobby Rydell and Lou Rawls.

USA

1 **The Three Bells**
The Browns

2 **Sea of Love**
Phil Phillips

3 **Sleep Walk**
Santo & Johnny

4 **Lavender Blue**
Sammy Turner

5 **I'm Gonna Get Married**
Lloyd Price

6 **What'd I Say**
Ray Charles

7 **A Big Hunk o' Love**
Elvis Presley

8 **There Goes My Baby**
The Drifters

9 **Red River Rock**
Johnny & The Hurricanes

10 **I Want to Walk You Home**
Fats Domino

UK

1 **Only Sixteen**
Craig Douglas

2 **Living Doll**
Cliff Richard

3 **Lonely Boy**
Paul Anka

4 **Lipstick on Your Collar**
Connie Francis

5 **China Tea**
Russ Conway

6 **Heart of a Man**
Frankie Vaughan

7 **Battle of New Orleans**
Lonnie Donegan

8 **Someone**
Johnny Mathis

9 **Here Comes Summer**
Jerry Keller

10 **Dream Lover**
Bobby Darin

Ray Charles. Inset: Cliff Richard

If 1959 will be remembered for anything, it may be the triptych of heavenly chorus classics – 'Dream Lover', 'Lonely Boy' and now Neil Sedaka's 'Oh! Carol', which even includes a wonderfully dreadful spoken section. Apparently written in love of fellow Brill Building writer Carole King, it goes to #9 in the US and spends four weeks at #3 in the UK. King immediately retaliates, releasing 'Oh Neil!' on Alpine, but without success.

'Some Kinda Earthquake' is Duane Eddy's fifth Top Forty record of the year, following 'Cannonball', 'The Lonely One', 'Yep' and the Top Ten 'Forty Miles of Bad Road'. Back in Phoenix for more recording, he probably notices a new face hanging round the studio. The Teddy Bears have drifted apart, and Phil Spector, eager to learn more about record production, has persuaded Hazlewood and Sill to let him hang out there. He reportedly drives everyone crazy with his endless questions.

The Miracles have their first minor hit with the Smokey Robinson-composed ballad 'Bad Girl'. Berry Gordy Jr, now increasingly involved with the group, has leased the record to Chess for better distribution. The setting up of his own Tamla-Motown label is now only a year away, and the Miracles will be one of his first signings.

In Britain Cliff Richard begins a seven-week spell at #1 with 'Travellin' Light'. The title perfectly describes the song – it's light, airy, with a sense of freedom that verges on the complacent. It's a long journey away from rock'n'roll, but it couldn't have existed without it.

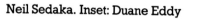

Neil Sedaka. Inset: Duane Eddy

USA

1 **Sleep Walk**
Santo and Johnny

2 **Mack the Knife**
Bobby Darin

3 **The Three Bells**
The Browns

4 **'Til I Kissed You**
The Everly Brothers

5 **I'm Gonna Get Married**
Lloyd Price

6 **Sea of Love**
Phil Phillips

7 **Put Your Head on My Shoulder**
Paul Anka

8 **Red River Rock**
Johnny & The Hurricanes

9 **Teen Beat**
Sandy Nelson

10 **Broken-Hearted Melody**
Sarah Vaughan

UK

1 **Only Sixteen**
Craig Douglas

2 **Here Comes Summer**
Jerry Keller

3 **Living Doll**
Cliff Richard

4 **'Til I Kissed You**
The Everly Brothers

5 **China Tea**
Russ Conway

6 **Forty Miles of Bad Road**
Duane Eddy

7 **Mona Lisa**
Conway Twitty

8 **Lonely Boy**
Paul Anka

9 **Just a Little Too Much**
Ricky Nelson

10 **Three Bells**
The Browns

Alan 'No one paid me to play these' Freed. Inset: Marty Robbins

USA

1 **Mack the Knife**
Bobby Darin

2 **Mr Blue**
The Fleetwoods

3 **Put Your Head on My Shoulder**
Paul Anka

4 **Don't You Know**
Della Reese

5 **Teen Beat**
Sandy Nelson

6 **Lonely Street**
Andy Williams

7 **Deck of Cards**
Wink Martindale

8 **Primrose Lane**
Jerry Wallace

9 **Just Ask Your Heart**
Frankie Avalon

10 **Poison Ivy**
The Coasters

UK

1 **Travellin' Light**
Cliff Richard

2 **Mack the Knife**
Bobby Darin

3 **Sea of Love**
Marty Wilde

4 **Red River Rock**
Johnny and The Hurricanes

5 **'Til I Kissed You**
The Everly Brothers

6 **Three Bells**
The Browns

7 **Makin' Love**
Floyd Robinson

8 **Put Your Head on My Shoulder**
Paul Anka

9 **What Do You Want to Make Those Eyes at Me For?**
Emile Ford

10 **Broken Hearted Melody**
Sarah Vaughan

A year of persistent probing by the authorities finally pays off, and the payola chickens begin heading home to roost, 12 months after *Billboard*'s initial warning. On the 20th Alan Freed, who has done as much as anyone over the last five years to create the climate in which rock'n'roll could flourish, refuses to swear that he has never accepted such payments, and is fired from WABC TV. Within ten days, having lost other radio and TV positions, he will be admitting his career has gone 'down the drain'. He won't be the only one. On the same day *Billboard* guesses that at least 25 other DJs are headed down the same chute.

As if in sympathy, Toni Fisher's 'The Big Hurt' enters the charts on its way to #3. It's notable for its Latin lilt, the Mickey Spillane-ish title and for being one of the first records to use sound phasing. A week later it's joined by Marty Robbins' 'El Paso', which will reach the top. Like Johnny Horton, Robbins is basically a country artist who uses material with a wider appeal, most notably gunfighter ballads like this.

Also moving towards the mainstream, Cliff Richard has his second film, *Expresso Bongo*, premièred in London on the 27th. In it he is imaginatively cast in the role of a teenage rock star.

Of course, Elvis will never go Middle of the Road. RCA says so. He won't change his style when he leaves the Army in March, a spokesman says. So it's official.

Two stars have dominated the R&B charts in 1959 to an extent hardly reflected in the pop charts. Between them Brook Benton and Lloyd Price have occupied the #1 spot for 27 weeks, with three chart-toppers each. Brook Benton's smoky-voiced ballads will do almost as well again in 1960.

In the UK relative newcomer Adam Faith is at #1 with 'What Do You Want', the first of many simple pop hits sung in his breathless Hollyish style. Not surprisingly, Bobby Vee covers the song in America, but without much success.

On the 15th the Everlys record outside Nashville and with strings, both for the first time – cutting the French song 'Let It Be Me' in New York. It reaches #7 in America, but in Britain is their smallest hit for a while. After almost three years the Brothers are considering leaving Cadence for either RCA or the about-to-be-established Warner Brothers label.

Middle America finally has its revenge on Chuck Berry for his theft of its children. Charged with transporting a minor, an Apache Indian girl, over a state line for immoral purposes, Berry counter-claims that he hired her as hat-check girl for his nightclub, was unaware of her age and, in any case, fired her as soon as he suspected her of prostitution. Eventually, according to most accounts, he will serve two years in prison.

The whole affair is still shrouded in mystery but, whatever the truth, Berry is effectively removed from an active role in music for the best part of five years. During that period his earlier work will continue to exert an enormous influence on, among others, the Beatles, the Stones, Dylan and the Beach Boys.

Sweet little thirteen? Chuck Berry holds his knees together.

USA

1 **Mack the Knife**
Bobby Darin

2 **Don't You Know**
Della Reese

3 **Mr Blue**
The Fleetwoods

4 **Heartaches by the Number**
Guy Mitchell

5 **In the Mood**
Ernie Fields

6 **So Many Ways**
Brook Benton

7 **Put Your Head on My Shoulder**
Paul Anka

8 **We Got Love**
Bobby Rydell

9 **Be My Guest**
Fats Domino

10 **Seven Little Girls**
Paul Evans & The Curls

UK

1 **What Do You Want**
Adam Faith

2 **What Do You Want to Make Those Eyes at Me For?**
Emile Ford

3 **Travellin' Light**
Cliff Richard

4 **Oh Carol**
Neil Sedaka

5 **Red River Rock**
Johnny & The Hurricanes

6 **Mack the Knife**
Bobby Darin

7 **Seven Little Girls Sitting in the Back Seat**
The Avons

8 **Teen Beat**
Sandy Nelson

8 **Put Your Head on My Shoulder**
Paul Anka

10 **'Til I Kissed You**
The Everly Brothers

1960

1960 was the year of marking time. No great new star burst forth, though two of rock'n'roll's older children – Brenda Lee and Roy Orbison – finally made it through to the big time after long apprenticeships. Significantly both hit #1 for the first time with ballads, not the rock'n'roll they'd cut their musical teeth on.

Elvis returned from the Army, prompting some to indulge in the illusion that he could roll back time on his own. TV shows with Sinatra, a clutch of Neapolitan ballads and the first of many bad movies proved otherwise – the King, though still capable of the exceptional, was mostly content to deliver no more than his contract stipulated.

Something new was needed, but Spector was still learning, Motown still gestating, and Liverpool's Cavern only just opening to rock'n'roll groups. In the meantime the established stars honed their skills, and the occasional one-hit-wonder flared briefly and disappeared. And there were the fads – death discs, instrumentals, the beginning of the dance craze. The old music was everywhere in the flesh, but harder to find in spirit.

The Everly Brothers

73

On the night of the 8th, Eddie Cochran makes his last recordings at Los Angeles' Goldstar Studio, with Crickets Sonny Curtis on guitar and Jerry Allison on drums. One of the songs is 'Three Steps to Heaven', notable not only for the future irony of its title, but also, in the restrained vocal, lush semi-acoustic strumming and Holly-like lead, for its demonstration of Cochran's continuing innovative power as a musician.

The following day he flies to Britain for the tour he's co-headlining with Gene Vincent.

The current song leading the Top Ten in the UK when he arrives is Emile Ford's 'What Do You Want to Make Those Eyes at Me For?' Ford is the first native black to hold that position.

The Big Bopper has a posthumous American #1 with his composition 'Running Bear'. Recorded by Johnny Preston more than a year earlier, it has Indian sounds contributed by the Bopper himself.

Jimmy Jones has been around since the mid-'50s, singing lead for several groups before launching a solo career that has, until now, not been notably successful. The falsetto-dominated 'Handyman' will reach #2, the follow-up 'Good Timin'' #3.

Brook Benton continues his R&B chart success, duetting with Dinah Washington on 'Baby (You've Got What It Takes)'. This will spend eight weeks at #1, the follow-up 'A Rockin' Good Way' a further five. Later in the year Benton's solo release 'Kiddio' will be #1 for nine weeks.

Meanwhile Sam Cooke signs for RCA and another singer with a voice you can pour, Jim Reeves, enters the charts with what will be his biggest hit, 'He'll Have to Go'. It's a fitting epitaph for the month. Cochran, Cooke, Reeves and Washington will all be dead before the decade is half over.

Dinah Washington, without Brook Benton, her partner in two huge successes this year

USA

1 **Why?**
Frankie Avalon

2 **El Paso**
Marty Robbins

3 **The Big Hurt**
Toni Fisher

4 **It's Time to Cry**
Paul Anka

5 **Way Down Yonder**
Freddie Cannon

6 **Heartaches by the Number**
Guy Mitchell

7 **Among My Souvenirs**
Connie Francis

8 **Mack the Knife**
Bobby Darin

9 **Hound Dog Man**
Fabian

10 **Pretty Blue Eyes**
Steve Lawrence

UK

1 **What Do You Want to Make Those Eyes at Me For?**
Emile Ford

2 **What Do You Want**
Adam Faith

3 **Oh Carol**
Neil Sedaka

4 **Seven Little Girls Sitting in the Back Seat**
The Avons

5 **Johnny Staccato Theme**
Elmer Bernstein

6 **Little White Bull**
Tommy Steele

7 **Bad Boy**
Marty Wilde

8 **Reveille Rock**
Johnny & The Hurricanes

9 **Travellin' Light**
Cliff Richard

10 **Some Kind-a-Earthquake**
Duane Eddy

USA

1 **Running Bear**
Johnny Preston

2 **Teen Angel**
Mark Dinning

3 **El Paso**
Marty Robbins

4 **Where or When**
Dion & The Belmonts

5 **Go Jimmy Go**
Jimmy Clanton

6 **Why**
Frankie Avalon

7 **Handy Man**
Jimmy Jones

8 **The Big Hurt**
Toni Fisher

9 **Way Down Yonder**
Freddie Cannon

10 **Pretty Blue Eyes**
Steve Lawrence

UK

1 **Why?**
Anthony Newley

2 **A Voice in the Wilderness**
Cliff Richard

3 **Starry-eyed**
Michael Holliday

4 **Way Down Yonder**
Freddie Cannon

5 **Heartaches by the Number**
Guy Mitchell

6 **Poor Me**
Adam Faith

7 **What Do You Want to Make Those Eyes at Me For?**
Emile Ford

8 **Expresso Bongo (E.P.)**
Cliff Richard

9 **Pretty Blue Eyes**
Craig Douglas

10 **Summer Set**
Acker Bilk

'My baby whispers in my ear' – Brenda Lee hits the big time at last

In the UK Anthony Newley takes over the #1 spot with his cover version of Frankie Avalon's US #1 'Why?' Newley, an actor as much as a singer, has started his recording career the previous year almost by accident – playing a rock'n'roll star in a film, and finding himself with a hit EP on his hands. Since then he's gone to #6 with a cover version of Lloyd Price's 'Personality' (US #2). 'Why?' marks a turn towards balladry which will take him through several more hits and back into the theatrical musical mainstream.

Almost four years after receiving her first recording contract, Brenda Lee, now at the ripe old age of 15, enters the Top Forty for the first time with 'Sweet Nothin's'. Lee's astonishing voice, with its strange blend of awesome power and teasing sexuality, makes the other popular white female singers of the time – most notably Connie Francis – sound decidedly torpid in comparison.

In the US 'Teen Angel' is #1 for two weeks. It's not the first 'death disc' by any means, but it does announce a black – even morbid – patch in the genre with its ludicrous tale of the girl who loses her wedding ring in the car stalled on the railroad track and goes back for it at the wrong moment.

A real death happens this month – Jesse Belvins dies in a Los Angeles car smash, aged 26. Best known to the wider pop audience as composer of 'Earth Angel', Belvins has had R&B hits as a solo artist and with a number of different doo-wop groups over a seven-year period.

The fact that 'Theme from A Summer Place' by the Percy Faith Orchestra is sitting at the top of the US charts can only increase, if that is possible, the sense of expectation surrounding Elvis Presley's release from the US Army. On the 5th the long-expected moment arrives. He leaves Fort Dix, New Jersey, and returns to Memphis by train.

On the 20th he goes to Nashville for a recording session. Scotty Moore is on guitar, but Bill Black, enjoying chart success with his own combo, has been replaced by Floyd Cramer on piano. Of the six songs recorded 'Stuck on You' and 'Fame and Fortune' are chosen for rush-release as the new single. So far, so good.

On the 23rd Elvis travels by train to Miami much in the style of a campaigning US President, except that he doesn't bore the adoring throngs with speeches. The aim of the trip is to make the TV special Colonel Parker has set up with, of all people, Frank Sinatra.

The show is recorded on the 26th. Elvis sings both sides of the single, and swaps songs with Ol' Blue Eyes – 'Witchcraft' for 'Love Me Tender'. His fee is $125,000, but who's to say what it costs him in the long run.

On the 14th Sam Cooke, who has recently joined Elvis on RCA, begins the first of three tours of the West Indies with a concert in Jamaica's Montego Bay. Large and ecstatic audiences will greet him over the next two weeks, and his vocal style will heavily influence young West Indian singers like Bob Marley and Jimmy Cliff.

USA

1 **Theme From A Summer Place**
Percy Faith
2 **Handy Man**
Jimmy Jones
3 **He'll Have to Go**
Jim Reeves
4 **Teen Angel**
Mark Dinning
5 **What in the World's Come over You**
Jack Scott
6 **Beyond the Sea**
Bobby Darin
7 **Running Bear**
Johnny Preston
8 **Let It Be Me**
The Everly Brothers
9 **Baby**
Brook Benton and Dinah Washington
10 **Wild One**
Bobby Rydell

UK

1 **Poor Me**
Adam Faith
2 **Running Bear**
Johnny Preston
3 **Why?**
Anthony Newley
4 **A Voice in the Wilderness**
Cliff Richard
5 **Slow Boat to China**
Emile Ford
6 **Way Down Yonder**
Freddie Cannon
7 **Delaware**
Perry Como
8 **Pretty Blue Eyes**
Craig Douglas
9 **Be Mine**
Lance Fortune
10 **Beyond the Sea**
Bobby Darin

Elvis – on his way out of the US Army

On the 3rd the Everly Brothers start their first British tour. They have recently signed to Warner Brothers for a reported $1 million, and released Don's 'Cathy's Clown' as the new label's first single. In the US the record holds #1 for five weeks, in the UK, bolstered by the tour, nine weeks. The record has the fuller, warmer sound typical of the early Warner recordings, a sound which they will further refine over the next two years, creating a body of music which many regard as their best.

Billy Fury's first album, the 10-inch *Sound of Fury*, is released. Almost all the songs are self-penned – Fury is the only major British star of this period writing his own songs.

There aren't many more Americans. Eddie Cochran's UK tour has proved so successful that he's invited to

do another, starting almost immediately. He and co-star Gene Vincent decide to have a few days back in the States between tours, and it's arranged that they'll take a late train from Bristol to London after the final gig.

But at the last minute they decide to go by road instead. Early in the morning of the 17th their car blows a tyre and swerves into a lamp post. Eddie Cochran is thrown against the roof of the car, and dies later that day in a Bath hospital from the head injuries he has sustained. Fiancée Sharon Sheeley, Gene Vincent and the driver all escape with injuries.

'Three Steps to Heaven' will follow 'Cathy's Clown' at #1, and singles will continue to be released for several years, but Cochran, like Holly before him, leaves behind the impression that he was only just getting started.

Eddie Cochran during one of his
last performances

USA

1 **Theme from A Summer Place**
Percy Faith

2 **Wild One**
Bobby Rydell

3 **He'll Have to Go**
Jim Reeves

4 **Puppy Love**
Paul Anka

5 **Sweet Nothin's**
Brenda Lee

6 **Baby**
Brook Benton and Dinah
Washington

7 **Handy Man**
Jimmy Jones

8 **Harbour Lights**
The Platters

9 **Forever**
Little Dippers

10 **O Dio Mio**
Annette

UK

1 **My Old Man's a Dustman**
Lonnie Donegan

2 **Running Bear**
Johnny Preston

3 **Fall in Love with You**
Cliff Richard

4 **Theme from A Summer Place**
Percy Faith

5 **Delaware**
Perry Como

6 **What in the World's Come
over You**
Jack Scott

7 **Fings Ain't What They
Used to Be**
Max Bygraves

8 **Poor Me**
Adam Faith

9 **Handy Man**
Jimmy Jones

10 **Do You Mind?**
Anthony Newley

Alan Freed and seven other DJs are indicted on payola charges by a Federal Grand Jury. Freed pleads not guilty and a trial is set for September. Dick Clark, however, comes out of it all smelling of roses. Or almost. 'You're not the inventor of the system, or even its architect,' the payola subcommittee chairman tells Clark, who seems just as implicated as everyone else. 'Obviously you're a fine young man.'

Freed hasn't invented or designed the system either, but apparently he doesn't qualify as so obvious 'a fine young man' in the chairman's sense of the words.

Closer to music, it's announced in *Billboard* that Berry Gordy Jr, Detroit producer, songwriter and music publisher, is setting up his own record labels – Motown and Tamla. The first releases, by the Satintones and Barrett Strong, will follow in June and July.

Phil Spector's patron Lester Sill also has close links with Leiber and Stoller in New York, and the two veterans (now both 27) agree to take on the 19-year-old as a virtual apprentice. At the time they are absorbed in creating for the Drifters that large echo-laden sound, complete with Latin rhythms and innovative string arrangements, which distinguishes hits like 'There Goes My Baby' and 'Save the Last Dance for Me'. 'Wind tunnel rock' someone calls it. Spector has a front seat.

Ben E. King, meanwhile, leaves the Drifters to start a solo career. His first release, 'Spanish Harlem', will be co-written by Spector and Jerry Leiber.

Adam Faith – the British inheritor of the Holly vocal mannerisms

USA

1 **Stuck on You**
Elvis Presley

2 **Green Fields**
Brothers Four

3 **Sixteen Reasons**
Connie Stevens

4 **Sink the Bismarck**
Johnny Horton

5 **Old Lamplighter**
The Browns

6 **Night**
Jackie Wilson

7 **Cradle of Love**
Johnny Preston

8 **Let the Little Girl Dance**
Billy Bland

9 **Theme from A Summer Place**
Percy Faith

10 **Sweet Nuthin's**
Brenda Lee

UK

1 **Cathy's Clown**
The Everly Brothers

2 **Do You Mind?**
Anthony Newley

3 **Someone Else's Baby**
Adam Faith

4 **Fall in Love with You**
Cliff Richard

5 **Handy Man**
Jimmy Jones

6 **Shazam**
Duane Eddy

7 **Sweet Nothin's**
Brenda Lee

8 **Stuck on You**
Elvis Presley

9 **My Old Man's a Dustman**
Lonnie Donegan

10 **Standing on the Corner**
The King Brothers

1 **Cathy's Clown**
The Everly Brothers

2 **Stuck on You**
Elvis Presley

3 **Good Timin'**
Jimmy Jones

4 **He'll Have to Stay**
Jeanne Black

5 **Green Fields**
Brothers Four

6 **Night**
Jackie Wilson

7 **Paper Roses**
Anita Bryant

8 **Sixteen Reasons**
Connie Stevens

9 **Burning Bridges**
Jack Scott

10 **Cradle of Love**
Johnny Preston

UK

1 **Cathy's Clown**
The Everly Brothers

2 **Cradle of Love**
Johnny Preston

3 **Shazam**
Duane Eddy

4 **Handy Man**
Jimmy Jones

5 **Sweet Nothin's**
Brenda Lee

6 **Three Steps to Heaven**
Eddie Cochran

7 **Mama/Robot Man**
Connie Francis

8 **Someone Else's Baby**
Adam Faith

9 **I Wanna Go Home**
Lonnie Donegan

10 **Footsteps**
Steve Lawrence

Roy Orbison's 'Only the Lonely' enters the US charts. Since leaving Sun in 1958 Orbison has cut one unsuccessful single for RCA and moved to the smaller Monument label. The first two singles, 'Paper Boy' and 'Uptown', have been minor hits; 'Only the Lonely', written by Orbison and long-time collaborator Joe Melson, will go to #2 in the US and #1 in Britain. The song, a rhythmic ballad, was written with Elvis in mind and turned down by the Everlys, but its pace and mood perfectly suit Orbison's peculiar voice, with its unique blend of white country melancholy and black blues emotiveness. The arrangement, with its close-to-parody doo-wop style backing, is also masterly. More than four years after signing with Sun, Orbison has found his musical niche.

Connie Francis's 'Everybody's Somebody's Fool' is her sixteenth entry on the US charts, and will be the first of her three #1s. Also headed for the top is the Hollywood Argyles' bizarre 'Alley Oop', produced by LA jack-of-all-musical trades, Kim Fowley. In the UK Adam Faith's double-sider 'Made You'/'Johnny Comes Marching Home' is on the way to being his fourth record in the top three in six months.

In Liverpool the Cavern Club begins allowing stage-

Connie Francis with big cat motif

time to rock'n'roll groups. On the 6th, one of the local groups, the Silver Beatles – recently reformed from the defunct Quarrymen with Lennon, McCartney, George Harrison, Stuart Sutcliffe and Pete Best – shares a gig in nearby Wallasey with another, Gerry and the Pacemakers.

Instrumentals seem to be suddenly popular. The Ventures, a two-guitar, bass and drums line-up, have their first US entry with 'Walk Don't Run'. The rolling sound looks forward to Californian surf music, and the heavy use of tremolo arm on the lead guitar's melody line anticipates almost every pop guitar solo of the coming decade.

The tremolo also dominates Hank B. Marvin's playing on the Shadows' first UK hit without Cliff Richard. 'Apache' goes to #1 in the UK, one notch ahead of a third instrumental, Duane Eddy's 'Because They're Young'. This, the theme from a movie starring Dick Clark and Tuesday Weld, will be Eddy's biggest hit on both sides of the Atlantic, but the aggressive drive of his earlier successes is notably absent. Hazlewood and Eddy have used strings for the first time, almost eclipsing the guitar.

In the States Lloyd Price has the last major hit of a run going back eight years with 'Question'. Brian Hyland has the first of a much shorter run with the novelty 'Itsy Bitsy Teenie Weenie Yellow Polkadot Bikini'. Though the record goes to #1, Hyland's voice will be displayed to better effect on two classic ballads in 1962.

Brenda Lee also has a first US #1 with the two-handkerchief ballad 'I'm Sorry'. The hard rocking 'B' side 'That's All You Gotta Do' reaches #6 on its own account.

USA

1 **Everybody's Somebody's Fool**
Connie Francis
2 **Cathy's Clown**
The Everly Brothers
3 **Alley-Oop**
Hollywood Argyles
4 **Burning Bridges**
Jack Scott
5 **Because They're Young**
Duane Eddy
6 **I'm Sorry**
Brenda Lee
7 **A Rockin' Good Way**
Dinah Washington and Brook Benton
8 **Paper Roses**
Anita Bryant
9 **Good Timin'**
Jimmy Jones
10 **Swinging School**
Bobby Rydell

UK

1 **Good Timin'**
Jimmy Jones
2 **Mama/Robot Man**
Connie Francis
3 **Three Steps to Heaven**
Eddie Cochran
4 **Ain't Misbehavin'**
Tommy Bruce
5 **Cathy's Clown**
The Everly Brothers
6 **What a Mouth**
Tommy Steele
7 **Please Don't Tease**
Cliff Richard
8 **Made You/When Johnny Comes Marching Home**
Adam Faith
9 **Angela Jones**
Michael Cox
10 **Shakin' All Over**
Johnny Kidd

Despite more than half a decade's R&B success Ray Charles has only had one Top Twenty entry on the pop chart. On the 3rd, perhaps sensing that a change of label will change his luck, he signs for ABC-Paramount.

The Shadows at a Wembley Poll-winners' Concert

You have to look sensitive, but not actually ill. Brian Hyland (inset) succeeds, Johnny Burnette fails.

Since the Sinatra show, Elvis Presley has recorded the songs for two more singles and the album *Elvis is Back*, shot the movie *G. I. Blues* and recorded the soundtrack album, had his tonsils out, and started filming *Flaming Star*.

The omens are decidedly mixed. The first album has some vintage Elvis, the second album next to none. *G. I. Blues* has him going through the paces, *Flaming Star* has him acting. The next single release, though, is an unmitigated disaster for lovers of rock'n'roll. 'It's Now or Never' is the old Italian song 'O Sole Mio', and Elvis simply performs it straight. The voice is as beautiful as ever, but there's no life, no energy, no challenge in the record. It's an enormous hit.

In Britain copyright problems hold up 'It's Now or Never', and the American 'B' side, 'A Mess of Blues', is paired with the album track 'Girl of My Best Friend' for local release. But it's only a temporary respite – 'It's Now or Never' will appear in November, enter the chart at #1, and stay there for nine weeks.

Rock'n'roll is no longer the name of the game. Johnny Burnette, who's been keeping the faith with and without brother Dorsey for five years, finally hits the big-time with 'Dreamin'', a gorgeous rollicking ballad complete with strings.

The Beatles, no longer Silver, play abroad for the first time, starting what will become a three-month gig at the Indra Club, Hamburg.

The American magazine *Seventeen* reports that the average teenage girl listens to the radio for 2 hours 13 minutes and plays records for 2 hours 12 minutes each day.

Sam Cooke's 'Chain Gang' is climbing both pop and R&B charts on its way to #2. It's his second RCA single, and the first of 18 Top Forty entries over the next five years. Though something of a novelty record with its groaning prisoners' chorus, 'Chain Gang' is also a fine showcase for Cooke's 'sweet soul' voice.

Less of a novelty, but rather more controversially, Ricky Valance enters the UK charts with his cover of Ray Peterson's American 'death disc' success, 'Tell Laura I Love Her'. In the song Laura's boyfriend Tommy has decided to cut down the waiting time for ring money by winning it in a stock car race. It's a bad decision. Since British Decca have scrapped 25,000 copies of Peterson's version on grounds of taste, Valance has a free run at the #1 spot.

At the top of the US list Elvis Presley gives way to Chubby Checker's new version of Hank Ballard's 'The Twist'. It's obviously all down to timing – Checker will go to #1 and set in motion the two years of dance crazes to be so lovingly portrayed in the '80s cult movie *Hairspray*. His name seems to have been put together by looking up Fats and Domino in a thesaurus.

Ike Turner has been around as performer, arranger and producer for nearly 10 years, working with such luminaries as B. B. King, Bobby 'Blue' Bland and Howlin' Wolf. His first single made with his 21-year-old wife Tina, 'A Fool in Love', is on its way up the R&B chart.

USA

1 **It's Now or Never**
Elvis Presley

2 **Walk Don't Run**
The Ventures

3 **The Twist**
Chubby Checker

4 **I'm Sorry**
Brenda Lee

5 **Volare**
Bobby Rydell

6 **Itsy Bitsy Teenie Weenie Yellow Polkadot Bikini**
Brian Hyland

7 **Finger Poppin' Time**
Hank Ballard & The Midnighters

8 **Mission Bell**
Donnie Brooks

9 **Only the Lonely**
Roy Orbison

10 **In My Little Corner of the World**
Anita Bryant

UK

1 **Apache**
The Shadows

2 **Because They're Young**
Duane Eddy

3 **The Girl of My Best Friend /A Mess of Blues**
Elvis Presley

4 **Please Don't Tease**
Cliff Richard

5 **When Will I be Loved**
The Everly Brothers

6 **Everybody's Somebody's Fool**
Connie Francis

7 **Shakin' All Over**
Johnny Kidd

8 **If She Should Come to You**
Anthony Newley

9 **Tie Me Kangaroo Down Sport**
Rolf Harris

10 **Tell Laura I Love Her**
Ricky Valance

Chubby Checker, on his way to the top with 'The Twist'

On the 27th, in the middle of the week which sees his penultimate record with the Drifters ('Save the Last Dance for Me') reach the US #1 spot, Ben E. King records his first solo sides in New York. Leiber and Stoller are producing, Phil Spector helping out. Four songs are recorded, three of Spector's (including 'Spanish Harlem' and 'First Taste of Love') and

the classic 'Stand by Me'.
'Spanish Harlem'/'First Taste of Love' will be issued as the first single, and its success will do a lot for Spector's confidence and reputation. At around this time he is asked to produce Ray Peterson's follow-up to 'Tell Laura I Love Her', a version of the traditional 'Corinne Corinna'. He works wonders, showing a feel for audio perspective before most

people have heard of it. The record goes to #9, and there's no Leiber and Stoller to share the glory.

A world away from such sophistication, Gary U. S. Bonds cuts 'New Orleans' in the back room of a Norfolk music store. The recording is such a mess, lacking any instrument separation, that it sounds like a party going on. For that very reason the record will be a huge hit, and

an influential one where people like Spector are concerned. The message is clear – the aim is no longer the accurate reproduction of sounds, but their creation.

In the charts, ballads seem to hold sway. Brenda Lee reaches #1 with 'I Want to be Wanted', Ray Charles is on his way with 'Georgia on My Mind'. Dion and the Belmonts split up, as if in recognition that an era is winding down.

Ray Charles on his way to several huge hits with countrified soul ballads, like 'Georgia on My Mind'

USA

1 **My Heart Has a Mind of Its Own**
Connie Francis

2 **Chain Gang**
Sam Cooke

3 **Mr Custer**
Larry Verne

4 **The Twist**
Chubby Checker

5 **A Million to One**
Jimmy Charles

6 **Save the Last Dance for Me**
The Drifters

7 **It's Now or Never**
Elvis Presley

8 **Walk Don't Run**
The Ventures

9 **So Sad**
The Everly Brothers

10 **Theme from The Apartment**
Ferrante & Teicher

UK

1 **Tell Laura I Love Her**
Ricky Valance

2 **Nine Times out of Ten**
Cliff Richard

3 **Only the Lonely**
Roy Orbison

4 **How about That**
Adam Faith

5 **Apache**
The Shadows

6 **The Girl of My Best Friend /A Mess of Blues**
Elvis Presley

7 **So Sad/Lucille**
The Everly Brothers

8 **Because They're Young**
Duane Eddy

9 **Walk, Don't Run**
The Ventures

10 **Please Help Me I'm Falling**
Hank Locklin

USA

1 **Save the Last Dance for Me**
The Drifters

2 **I Want to be Wanted**
Brenda Lee

3 **My Heart Has a Mind of Its Own**
Connie Francis

4 **The Twist**
Chubby Checker

5 **Chain Gang**
Sam Cooke

6 **You Talk Too Much**
Joe Jones

7 **Devil or Angel**
Bobby Vee

8 **Let's Think About Living**
Bob Luman

9 **Poetry in Motion**
Johnny Tillotson

10 **Georgia on My Mind**
Ray Charles

UK

1 **It's Now or Never**
Elvis Presley

2 **Only the Lonely**
Roy Orbison

3 **As Long as He Needs Me**
Shirley Bassey

4 **Rocking Goose**
Johnny and The Hurricanes

5 **Nine Times Out of Ten**
Cliff Richard

6 **So Sad/Lucille**
The Everly Brothers

7 **Let's Think about Living**
Bob Luman

8 **Dreamin'**
Johnny Burnette

9 **How about That**
Adam Faith

10 **Walk, Don't Run**
The John Barry Seven

Now on Vee Jay, soul singer Jerry Butler enters the charts with 'He Will Break Your Heart', a song he has co-written with Curtis Mayfield. It's the beginning of a good run for the man they call 'The Iceman' – partly on account of his super-cool stage persona, partly because he has ambitions to be an ice sculptor. Mayfield, meanwhile, has secured a record deal for the Impressions with ABC-Paramount, but it will be another three years before the group really takes off.

Hank Ballard and the Midnighters have hit a new purple patch despite losing out to Chubby Checker's version of 'The Twist'. 'Let's Go, Let's Go, Let's Go' will be R&B #1 for four weeks, and their second Top Ten hit in the pop chart in three months.

Duane Eddy and Lee Hazlewood part company, for reasons that remain obscure. Despite losing his co-writer and producer, Eddy will continue to have hits through 1961–2, albeit of a less resounding and less memorable nature.

On the 5th Johnny Horton, currently on his way to #4 with the movie theme song 'North to Alaska', is killed in a car crash. Like Hank Williams, he meets his death after playing a last gig at the Skyline club in Austin, Texas. More unusually, he leaves behind the same widow.

On the 10th Gregg Allman gets a guitar for his thirteenth birthday. He and older brother Duane will be forming their first group before the next year is out.

Jerry Butler, now divorced from the Impressions

I t was to have been the year of the King's return, and in a way it has been. The December charts certainly suggest as much: 'It's Now or Never' and 'Are You Lonesome Tonight?' are #1 in the UK and US respectively throughout the month, and the homecoming album *G. I. Blues* is top of the album chart for most of it. Elvis Presley is going to be in a lot of stockings this Christmas.

But in another way Elvis has not returned, or at least not the Elvis that went away. Like the music he helped to shape, Elvis has grown older and more successful. Both man and music are now sufficiently established to take risks, but their very establishment makes them less inclined to take them. The fans don't seem to mind, or to have noticed.

The stars who have come to prominence over the last two or three years are still full of music. The Everly Brothers, to name but two, have had a great year, producing several excellent singles and two first-rate albums. And there's always the surprises, records that just spring from nowhere, sounding like nothing else ever sounded. Rosie and the Originals' 'Angel Baby' enters the charts on its way to #5. Rosie sounds about ten years old, and so desperately in love you wonder how she can sing.

Pop's future is still practising in the wings. Motown's Mary Wells makes her R&B chart debut with 'Bye Bye Baby', and on the 31st the Miracles' 'Shop Around' is released. It will be the Detroit company's first million-seller. In Liverpool the Beatles play a 'Welcome Home' concert for their hometown fans after returning from Germany.

Mary Wells – one of the first Motown stars. Inset: Gary U.S. Bonds

USA

1 **Are You Lonesome Tonight**
Elvis Presley

2 **Last Date**
Floyd Cramer

3 **Stay**
Maurice Williams

4 **Poetry in Motion**
Johnny Tillotson

5 **A Thousand Stars**
Kathy Young & The Innocents

6 **New Orleans**
U.S. Bonds

7 **North to Alaska**
Johnny Horton

8 **Alone at Last**
Jackie Wilson

9 **Let's Go, Let's Go, Let's Go**
Hank Ballard & The
    Midnighters

10 **Georgia on My Mind**
Ray Charles

UK

1 **It's Now or Never**
Elvis Presley

2 **Save the Last Dance for Me**
The Drifters

3 **Man of Mystery/The Stranger**
The Shadows

4 **Strawberry Fair**
Anthony Newley

5 **Goodness Gracious Me**
Peter Sellers and
    Sophia Loren

6 **Rocking Goose**
Johnny and The Hurricanes

7 **My Heart Has a Mind of
    Its Own**
Connie Francis

8 **I Love You**
Cliff Richard

9 **As Long as He Needs Me**
Shirley Bassey

10 **Little Donkey**
Nina and Frederik

1961

1961 was a vintage year for singles. In retrospect it seems as if the practitioners of the pre-Beatles era somehow realized time was short, and decided to cram all the quality they could manage into 12 brief months. 'Runaway', 'Duke of Earl', 'Stand by Me', 'Poetry in Motion', 'Temptation', 'Take Good Care of My Baby', 'The Lion Sleeps Tonight', 'Crying', 'Will You Love Me Tomorrow', 'Blue Moon', 'Travelin' Man', 'Quarter to Three' . . . it's hard to think of another year so bursting with mainstream riches.

Certainly time was running out for the smooth, uncluttered and melodic balladry that had dominated the last few years. Motown began the year with its first million-seller and ended with its first #1. Phil Spector launched his own label, the Beach Boys came together and took their name. As Elvis gave up live performance, the Beatles played the Cavern for the first time. A young Bob Dylan arrived in Greenwich Village to begin the haunting of America.

Roy Orbison

Johnny Tillotson's 'Poetry in Motion' is Britain's first new #1 of the year. The song has that indefinable blend of qualities which makes for pop greatness – it's different without being too different, the melody is catchy yet remains interesting, and the lyrics mean something but don't require thought. The performance is satisfactory, but the identity of the singer is largely irrelevant – he serves the song, rather than the other way round.

The success of 'Poetry in Motion' is a fitting beginning to 1961, which will have more than its share of such classic singles. The softening of rock'n'roll's rough edges over the last few years may have corroded any art at the centre of the music's creation, but the crafting of great singles is perhaps now reaching its peak.

Billy Fury can see the writing on the wall. After 18 months of relative failure with his own (often excellent) compositions, he covers an American hit – Kathy Young and the Innocents' 'A Thousand Stars' – and at least makes the Top Twenty. The next cover, of Tony Orlando's Goffin-King number 'Halfway to Paradise', will establish him as a consistent Top Ten artist.

Elvis Presley's 'Are You Lonesome Tonight?' loses the American #1 spot and gains the British. He signs a new film contract with Hal Wallis, committing him to make at least one film a year for the next five. Quantity is obviously not going to be a problem.

Like an echo of the previous decade two doo-wop classics – the Five Satins' 'In The Still of the Night' and the Mello-Kings' 'Tonight Tonight' – make belated reappearances in the charts.

Billy Fury and the Tornadoes on stage

USA

1 **Are You Lonesome Tonight**
Elvis Presley

2 **Wonderland by Night**
Bert Kämpfert

3 **Last Date**
Floyd Cramer

4 **Exodus**
Ferrante & Teicher

5 **A Thousand Stars**
Kathy Young & The Innocents

6 **North to Alaska**
Johnny Horton

7 **Many Tears Ago**
Connie Francis

8 **You're Sixteen**
Johnny Burnette

9 **Angel Baby**
Rosie & The Originals

10 **Corrine Corrina**
Ray Peterson

UK

1 **Poetry in Motion**
Johnny Tillotson

2 **Save the Last Dance for Me**
The Drifters

3 **I Love You**
Cliff Richard

4 **It's Now or Never**
Elvis Presley

5 **Lonely Pup**
Adam Faith

6 **Perfidia**
The Ventures

7 **Strawberry Fair**
Anthony Newley

8 **Man of Mystery/The Stranger**
The Shadows

9 **Counting Teardrops**
Emile Ford

9 **Goodness Gracious Me**
Peter Sellers and
Sophia Loren

Another perfect single goes to #1 in the US. Indeed, with its haunting melody and simple evocative lyrics, many will come to regard 'Will You Love Me Tomorrow' as *the* perfect pop song. It will be the first of half a dozen Top Ten hits for the Shirelles, a black all-girl group from New York. Their success is ground-breaking – such groups will become as dominant a musical force over the next five years as their male counterparts have been over the last ten.

'Will You Love Me Tomorrow' is also the first #1 for songwriting husband-and-wife team Gerry Goffin and Carole King. Between now and their separation in 1967 the pair will write numerous million-sellers for a large number of artists, including one for Carole herself.

Another songwriter, Gene Pitney, makes his chart debut with '(I Wanna) Love My Life Away'. Buoyed with the success of his compositions 'Rubber Ball' and 'Today's Teardrops' (hits for Bobby Vee and Roy Orbison) Pitney has quit university and recorded the song on a four-track at a cost of $30, singing all the parts and playing most of the instruments. The recording of his third single later in the year will be a very different financial story.

The Miracles' 'Shop Around', written by Berry Gordy Jr and Smokey Robinson, goes to #1 on the R&B chart, #2 on the pop chart, and becomes Motown's first million-seller. Smokey Robinson's high emotive voice will be confined to his own and Miracles' records; the record's heavily accented beat and bursting sense of energy will characterize most of the label's output over the coming decade.

USA

1 **Will You Love Me Tomorrow**
The Shirelles

2 **Calcutta**
Lawrence Welk

3 **Exodus**
Ferrante & Teicher

4 **Wonderland By Night**
Bert Kämpfert

5 **Shop Around**
The Miracles

6 **Angel Baby**
Rosie & The Originals

7 **Calendar Girl**
Neil Sedaka

8 **Emotions**
Brenda Lee

9 **Rubber Ball**
Bobby Vee

10 **Are You Lonesome Tonight**
Elvis Presley

UK

1 **Are You Lonesome Tonight**
Elvis Presley

2 **Sailor**
Petula Clark

3 **Pepe**
Duane Eddy

4 **Rubber Ball**
Bobby Vee

5 **Poetry in Motion**
Johnny Tillotson

6 **You're Sixteen**
Johnny Burnette

7 **Portrait of My Love**
Matt Monro

8 **Sailor**
Anne Shelton

9 **Counting Teardrops**
Emile Ford

10 **Rubber Ball**
Marty Wilde

'Will you still love me tomorrow?'
Gerry Goffin and Carole King in conversation

On the 10th Jeff Barry, co-writer of 'Tell Laura I Love Her', signs a ten-year contract with Trinity Music. The following year he will marry Ellie Greenwich, and between them they'll rival if not surpass Goffin and King, writing many of the girl-group records produced by Phil Spector at Philles and 'Shadow' Morton at Red Bird – including 'Then I Kissed Him', 'Be My Baby', 'River Deep, Mountain High' and 'Leader of the Pack'.

Like many American stars before them, the Everly Brothers are begining to do 'Ebony Eyes' ('the plane may have run into some turbulent weather . . .') only reaches #9 in the US, but tops the UK chart for four weeks.

The British chart has a familiar look to it, with the latest from local stalwarts (Cliff Richard, the Shadows, Adam Faith) and familiar Americans (Brenda Lee, Bobby Vee, Duane Eddy, Johnny and the Hurricanes) all highly placed. Plus, of course, Elvis Presley, whose 'Wooden Heart' succeeds the Everlys, giving him an unprecedented third consecutive #1. The man himself, in Hawaii to film

USA

1 **Pony Time**
Chubby Checker

2 **Calcutta**
Lawrence Welk

3 **There's a Moon Out Tonight**
Capris

4 **Surrender**
Elvis Presley

5 **Don't Worry**
Marty Robbins

6 **Dedicated to the One I Love**
The Shirelles

7 **Where the Boys Are**
Connie Francis

8 **Shop Around**
The Miracles

9 **Ebony Eyes**
The Everly Brothers

10 **Wheels**
The String-A-Longs

UK

1 **Walk Right Back/Ebony Eyes**
The Everly Brothers

2 **Are You Sure?**
The Allisons

3 **Sailor**
Petula Clark

4 **Will You Love Me Tomorrow**
The Shirelles

5 **Are You Lonesome Tonight**
Elvis Presley

6 **F.B.I.**
The Shadows

7 **Theme for a Dream**
Cliff Richard

8 **Riders in the Sky**
The Ramrods

9 **Who Am I?/This is It**
Adam Faith

10 **Rubber Ball**
Bobby Vee

better in Britain than at home. The pairing of the march-tempo 'Walk Right Back', written by Cricket Sonny Curtis, and the death-disc

Blue Hawaii, does a benefit concert on the 25th for the USS *Arizona* Memorial Fund. It will be his last live stage appearance for eight years.

On the other side of the world, as if in recompense, the Beatles tread the stage of the Cavern Club for the first time.

An invitation to the 1960s – a poster outside Liverpool's Cavern Club

The month begins with Elvis atop the US charts with another Italian ballad, 'Come Back to Sorrento', revamped as 'Surrender'. It's displaced by another updated standard, though 'updated' hardly does justice to the changes wrought on 'Blue Moon' by the Marcels. The mixed-race group from Pittsburgh doesn't so much perform the Rodgers-Hart standard as drive straight through it. 'Dang-de-dang-dang-de-dong-ding-de-dong-ding-blue-moon . . .'.

Only real class could compete with this, and Del Shannon's 'Runaway' is another of the year's pop classics – neat lyric, flowing melody, gimmicks (falsetto and organ break) perfectly integrated. Shannon, rarely for the period, even writes his own songs. Like 'Surrender' and 'Blue Moon', 'Runaway' will hit #1 on both sides of the Atlantic.

Nineteen-year-old Bob Zimmerman, now wearing the name Dylan, has been in New York less than three months when he makes his stage debut at Gerde's Folk City in Greenwich Village on the 11th. A fortnight later he makes his recording debut, playing harmonica on Harry Belafonte's 'Midnight Special'. His fee is $50.

The world has need of him. In Britain the BBC bans Craig Douglas's cover of Gene McDaniels's 'A Hundred Pounds of Clay' (on its way to US #3) on grounds of blasphemy. Apparently women are not manufactured out of building materials. The lyrics are revised, forelocks tugged, and Craig's version goes to UK #8.

USA

1 **Blue Moon**
The Marcels

2 **Apache**
Jorgen Ingmann

3 **Surrender**
Elvis Presley

4 **Pony Time**
Chubby Checker

5 **Dedicated to the One I Love**
The Shirelles

6 **Don't Worry**
Marty Robbins

7 **On the Rebound**
Floyd Cramer

8 **Walk Right Back**
The Everly Brothers

9 **Runaway**
Del Shannon

10 **But I Do**
Clarence Henry

UK

1 **Wooden Heart**
Elvis Presley

2 **Walk Right Back/Ebony Eyes**
The Everly Brothers

3 **Are You Sure?**
The Allisons

4 **Theme for a Dream**
Cliff Richard

5 **My Kind of Girl**
Matt Monro

6 **Lazy River**
Bobby Darin

7 **Exodus**
Ferranti and Teicher

8 **And the Heavens Cried**
Anthony Newley

8 **Will You Love Me Tomorrow**
The Shirelles

10 **Riders in the Sky**
The Ramrods

Del Shannon, courtesy of British Rail. Inset: The Shirelles

Billy Fury's 'Halfway to Paradise' is released in Britain, where it will prove his biggest hit yet, reaching #4. In the US Tony Orlando's original version of the Goffin-King song only reaches #39, and Orlando has to wait until the fall for his first and last Top Twenty success of the '60s, the powerful 'Bless You'. Nine years later he will reappear as one third of the highly successful Dawn.

The writer of 'Bless You', Barry Mann, is another of the Brill Building's star songwriters. He and new wife Cynthia Weill will write a string of million-sellers over the next decade, including several for the Crystals and Drifters, the Righteous Brothers' 'You've Lost That Loving Feeling' and the Animals' 'We Gotta Get Outta This Place'. Many of the couple's songs will be distinguished by what, for the time and the genre, is a rare sense of social protest.

Gladys Knight and the Pips have their first single out. Or singles. Because of a contractual dispute 'Every Beat of My Heart' is issued in two versions, one on Fury credited to Gladys, one on Vee Jay to the Pips, though exactly the same people have sung and played on each. The Vee Jay single does better, going to #6 on the pop chart, and following Ben E. King's 'Stand by Me' to the top of the R&B list.

The Beatles are also recording for the first time, with Polydor in Germany. Though ostensibly there to provide backing for Tony Sheridan, the boys also manage to record 'Ain't She Sweet' and 'Cry for a Shadow' without him.

USA

1 **Runaway**
Del Shannon

2 **Mother-In-Law**
Ernie K-Doe

3 **I've Told Every Little Star**
Linda Scott

4 **A Hundred Pounds of Clay**
Gene McDaniels

5 **Blue Moon**
Marcels

6 **But I Do**
Clarence Henry

7 **Take Good Care of Her**
Adam Wade

8 **One Mint Julep**
Ray Charles

9 **You Can Depend on Me**
Brenda Lee

10 **On the Rebound**
Floyd Cramer

UK

1 **You're Driving Me Crazy**
The Temperance Seven

2 **Blue Moon**
The Marcels

3 **Wooden Heart**
Elvis Presley

4 **Don't Treat Me like a Child**
Helen Shapiro

5 **On the Rebound**
Floyd Cramer

6 **Warpaint**
The Brook Brothers

7 **Theme from Dixie**
Duane Eddy

8 **A Hundred Pounds of Clay**
Craig Douglas

9 **Gee Whiz It's You**
Cliff Richard

10 **Lazy River**
Bobby Darin

Gladys Knight and the Pips, early in their career

In the US Roy Orbison's 'Running Scared' reaches #1. It establishes the definitive pattern for 'Big O' records – starting slow, smouldering like a fuse towards the falsetto crescendo, wringing every emotion there is to wring out of the listener, and leaving the song's protagonist either on the brink of romantic extinction or already contemplating the despairing reality. Another variation on the theme, the even better 'Crying', will make #2 four months later, in October.

On the 8th, on his 21st birthday, Ricky Nelson formally becomes plain Rick. He has another near-perfect double-sided hit climbing the charts – Jerry Fuller's 'Travelin' Man', which has been turned down by Sam Cooke, backed with Gene Pitney's 'Hello Mary Lou'. The two sides reach #1 and #9 in the US, together they go to #3 in Britain.

Also on the 8th, Elvis's seventh film, *Wild in the Country*, is premièred in Memphis. The original movie, with no songs and a screenplay by Clifford Odets, has obviously been intended as a serious dramatic effort, but unfortunately the reaction of critics and fans at pre-release screenings is overwhelmingly negative. Several songs are inserted.

Pat Boone's 'Moody River' follows 'Travelin' Man' at #1. A death disc *par excellence* ('your muddy water took my baby's life'), it's his sixth chart-topper and thirty-fourth Top Forty entry. There are four more of the latter to go.

Stuart Sutcliffe marries, leaves the Beatles and goes to study art in Hamburg. In New Jersey three men get prison sentences (one suspended) for the crime of record bootlegging. They're the first.

Rick Nelson, with new shortened name adorning his guitar

USA

1 **Travelin' Man**
Ricky Nelson
2 **Daddy's Home**
Shep & The Limelites
3 **Runnin' Scared**
Roy Orbison
4 **Mama Said**
The Shirelles
5 **Mother-In-Law**
Ernie K-Doe
6 **Runaway**
Del Shannon
7 **Breakin' in a Brand New Broken Heart**
Connie Francis
8 **A Hundred Pounds of Clay**
Gene McDaniels
9 **I Feel So Bad**
Elvis Presley
10 **Tragedy**
The Fleetwoods

UK

1 **Surrender**
Elvis Presley
2 **Runaway**
Del Shannon
3 **More Than I Can Say**
Bobby Vee
4 **The Frightened City**
The Shadows
5 **Blue Moon**
The Marcels
6 **On the Rebound**
Floyd Cramer
7 **You'll Never Know**
Shirley Bassey
8 **What'd I Say?**
Jerry Lee Lewis
9 **But I Do**
Clarence Frogman Henry
10 **Don't Treat Me like a Child**
Helen Shapiro

The Everly Brothers go to #1 in the UK with a revolutionary interpretation of the old Bing Crosby favourite, 'Temptation'. With ringing lead guitar and a female chorus that wails like a holdfull of galley slaves, it sounds unlike anything they've ever done before. Manager Wesley Rose has opposed the release, presumably for this very reason, and parted company with the Brothers. Unfortunately for the Everlys, the split with Rose will also deny them access to the Bryants' songs, and this at a time – a few months before they begin a period of military service – when they need all the good material they can get.

In America Gary U. S. Bonds is #1 for two weeks with his second party special, 'Quarter To Three', before giving way to a seven-week

run by the year's biggest hit, Bobby Lewis's 'Tossin' and Turnin''. The twist craze is still spreading like a plague, and infecting even adults in Philadelphia, according to a story in *Billboard*.

In the UK the George Mitchell Minstrels – white men made up as black – have the first of three consecutive chart-topping albums. Pat Boone is touring South Africa. Nelson Mandela is still at liberty.

In Liverpool the first issue of the fan magazine *Merseybeat* appears on the 6th, with an article by John Lennon entitled 'Being a Short Diversion on the Dubious Origins of Beatles'.

A new group is unveiled by Motown: Diana Ross, Florence Ballard and Mary Wilson, collectively known as the Supremes, have their first single, 'Buttered Popcorn', released on the 17th. It makes little impression.

USA

1 **Quarter to Three**
  U.S. Bonds
2 **Tossin' and Turnin'**
  Bobby Lewis
3 **Boll Weevil Song**
  Brook Benton
4 **Raindrops**
  Dee Clark
5 **The Writing on the Wall**
  Adam Wade
6 **Moody River**
  Pat Boone
7 **Travellin' Man**
  Ricky Nelson
8 **Every Beat of My Heart**
  The Pips
9 **Those Oldies but Goodies**
  Little Caesar & The Romans
10 **Yellow Bird**
  Arthur Lyman

UK

1 **Runaway**
  Del Shannon
2 **Surrender**
  Elvis Presley
3 **Temptation**
  The Everly Brothers
4 **Pasadena**
  The Temperance Seven
5 **A Girl like You**
  Cliff Richard
6 **Hello Mary Lou/Travellin' Man**
  Ricky Nelson
7 **Halfway to Paradise**
  Billy Fury
8 **But I Do**
  Clarence Frogman Henry
9 **The Frightened City**
  The Shadows
10 **You'll Never Know**
  Shirley Bassey

Yes, it's a quarter to three – U.S. Bonds. Inset: Del Shannon

USA

(Left) Boy preacher Solomon Burke and (right) habitual ignorer of health warnings, Gene Vincent

On the 2nd the Beatles start playing regularly at the Cavern Club in Liverpool. One of the songs they will eventually record, 'Please Mr Postman', is released by the Marvelettes on Tamla. It will be the first #1 for Berry Gordy Jr's corporation.

In the instrumental stakes the Shadows release 'Kon Tiki', which will be their third British #1. Johnny and the Hurricanes' run of success is coming to an end – they haven't had a US hit for eighteen months, and the double-sided 'Old Smokey'/ 'High Voltage' will be their last UK chart entry.

Gene Vincent, one of the few original rock'n'rollers still on the road, collapses from exhaustion during a British tour. His luck, always bad, will not improve, and a drinking problem will contribute to his premature death in 1971.

On the 24th Atlantic release their first Solomon Burke single, 'Just out of Reach (of My Two Open Arms)'. Burke has a long apprenticeship in gospel – singing professionally since the age of nine, having his own radio show, and performing as 'The Wonder Boy Preacher' on the national gospel circuit. Several years of recording mostly religious and sentimental ballads for Apollo and Singular have met with little success, but 'Just out of Reach' will go to #7 on the R&B chart, and usher in a series of performances on record that will prove crucial to the evolution of the Atlantic soul catalogue through the '60s.

UK

Another pair of classic pop singles dominates the charts – Bobby Vee's 'Take Good Care of My Baby' in the US and John Leyton's 'Johnny Remember Me' in the UK. Both are pure pop – all melody, atmosphere and teenage angst. It's easier to imagine the protagonists in tears than angry.

Ral Donner, best known as the Elvis Presley copyist *par excellence*, reaches #4 in the US with 'You Don't Know What You've Got'. The main difference between his records and the King's, in 1961, is that Donner's are generally superior. He sings them the way Elvis used to sing his before (in the opinion of a significant minority of his fans) selling out his talent for a mess of Neapolitan crooning and bad movies.

The slow mutation of the King into mere pop is creating space for new heroes. In California the Wilson parents go away, leaving their three sons and a couple of friends to practise being Beach Boys.

In New York the 20-year-old Bob Dylan starts a two-week run at Gerdes Folk City, and gets his first press review – Robert Shelton announcing in the *New York Times* that this 'cross between a beatnik and a choir boy' is 'bursting at the seams with talent'. In between shows, Dylan guests on friend Carolyn Hester's album, and in the process so impresses CBS producer John Hammond that he's given a record contract of his own.

USA

1 **Wooden Heart**
Joe Dowell

2 **Tossin' and Turnin'**
Bobby Lewis

3 **Michael**
The Highwaymen

4 **Last Night**
The Mar-Keys

5 **You Don't Know What You've Got**
Ral Donner

6 **I Like It Like That**
Chris Kenner

7 **School is Out**
U.S. Bonds

8 **Pretty Little Angel Eyes**
Curtis Lee

9 **Don't Bet Money Honey**
Linda Scott

10 **Hurt**
Timi Yuro

UK

1 **Johnny Remember Me**
John Leyton

2 **You Don't Know**
Helen Shapiro

3 **Reach for the Stars /Climb Every Mountain**
Shirley Bassey

4 **Romeo**
Petula Clark

5 **Well I Ask You**
Eden Kane

6 **Halfway to Paradise**
Billy Fury

7 **A Girl like You**
Cliff Richard

8 **Ain't Gonna Wash for a Week**
The Brook Brothers

9 **Cupid**
Sam Cooke

10 **Time**
Craig Douglas

Bob Dylan, the beatnik choirboy

USA

1 **Take Good Care of My Baby**
Bobby Vee

2 **The Mountain's High**
Dick and Deedee

3 **Cryin'**
Roy Orbison

4 **Hit the Road Jack**
Ray Charles

5 **Little Sister**
Elvis Presley

6 **Michael**
The Highwaymen

7 **Mexico**
Bob Moore

8 **You Must Have Been
a Beautiful Baby**
Bobby Darin

9 **Does Your Chewing Gum
Lose Its Flavor**
Lonnie Donegan

10 **Bristol Stomp**
The Dovells

UK

1 **Michael**
The Highwaymen

2 **Wild in the Country/I Feel
So Bad**
Elvis Presley

3 **Walkin' Back to Happiness**
Helen Shapiro

4 **Kon Tiki**
The Shadows

5 **Johnny Remember Me**
John Leyton

6 **Jealousy**
Billy Fury

7 **You'll Answer to Me**
Cleo Laine

8 **Wild Wind**
John Leyton

9 **Sucu Sucu**
Laurie Johnson

10 **You Don't Know**
Helen Shapiro

Joan Baez and Judy Collins release albums, their second and first respectively. For the moment both are recording only traditional material, but over the next five years each will do much to popularize the work of talented unknowns in the new folk field – singer-songwriters like Dylan, Phil Ochs, Leonard Cohen, Joni Mitchell and Randy Newman.

On the 21st Dylan records his first album. It contains only two of his own songs, the sardonic 'Talkin' New York' and elegiac 'Song to Woody'.

The session costs $400.

Musicor have been less frugal with Gene Pitney's new release, 'Every Breath I Take'. Produced by freelancing Phil Spector at a four-song session which costs an unheard-of $13,000, it features a grandiose falsetto climax which owes a great deal to Pitney's heavy nose-cold. The record only goes to #42.

In the meantime Spector and Lester Sill launch their own label, Philles, with 'There's No Other (Like My Baby)' by the Crystals, a black female quintet from New York. Though no classic, it will still reach #20.

In Detroit a new partnership is getting underway. Lamont Dozier has enjoyed little success as a singer, rather more as a songwriter; Brian Holland has been in at Motown from the beginning as a writer-producer. Sometime in the coming year Brian's brother Eddie will complete the most successful songwriting trio in history – with 19 million-sellers to show for their first ten years together.

Dick and Deedee will only have one, but 'The Mountain's High', cresting at #2, is one of the year's strangest records – two teenagers wailing about the geography of lost love, reduced to making demented bird noises as the music fades away.

The Crystals

According to *Billboard* the twist craze is now global, though the globe in question only seems to include the US, Britain and France. In the last-named, 45 twist records have been released, including versions of 'The Twist' by Johnny Hallyday and Richard Anthony which share the French #1 spot. In New York WOR-TV is showing twist lessons by Chubby Checker every hour on the hour. Sundry twist films are in the works, including the originally titled 'Twist Round the Clock' which will star Dion.

Dion's new single 'Runaround Sue' enters the US chart. Though pop seems to be getting softer, he seems to be moving in the opposite direction. Both 'Runaround Sue' and follow-up 'The Wanderer' (#1 and #2 respectively) have a harder sound and a harder message. When Dion sings about Sue 'going out with other guys', you know it's not exactly 'going out' he's talking about.

In Liverpool, record-shop manager Brian Epstein, his curiosity whetted by requests for Tony Sheridan and the Beatles' 'My Bonnie', goes to see the latter at the Cavern. Impressed, he introduces himself to Paul and George, and starts persuading them that he should be their manager. In New York Dylan plays the Carnegie Hall for the first time, to an audience of about 50, most of them friends.

On the 25th the Everlys are inducted into the Marine Corps for a six-month stint. In the US the Impressions have their first hit with 'Gypsy Woman'; in Britain 14-year-old Helen Shapiro has her second #1 in three months with 'Walkin' Back to Happiness'.

USA

1 **Runaround Sue**
Dion

2 **Bristol Stomp**
The Dovells

3 **Big Bad John**
Jimmy Dean

4 **Hit the Road Jack**
Ray Charles

5 **I Love How You Love Me**
Paris Sisters

6 **Sad Movies**
Sue Thompson

7 **Ya Ya**
Lee Dorsey

8 **Let's Get Together**
Hayley Mills

9 **The Fly**
Chubby Checker

10 **This Time**
Troy Shondell

UK

1 **Walkin' Back to Happiness**
Helen Shapiro

2 **His Latest Flame /Little Sister**
Elvis Presley

3 **When the Girl in Your Arms is the Girl in Your Heart**
Cliff Richard

4 **Big Bad John**
Jimmy Dean

5 **Hit the Road Jack**
Ray Charles

6 **Wild Wind**
John Leyton

7 **Mexicali Rose**
Karl Denver

8 **Sucu Sucu**
Laurie Johnson

9 **Take Five**
Dave Brubeck

10 **Michael**
The Highwaymen

Dion – now minus the Belmonts

In the wake of Dick and Deedee's 'The Mountain's High' come two more extraordinary one-off records. The Tokens' 'The Lion Sleeps Tonight' will be the first African folk song to top the American chart, though what remains of its cultural origins is a moot question. As the lead singer tells his love to sleep safe – the local lion is out for the count – an astonishing sound collage of spiralling falsettos, hup-hups, trills and tribal chants fills every available space on the record.

Gene Chandler's 'Duke of Earl' is equally original, and also bound for #1. A guard-of-honour chorus intones 'duke, duke, duke, duke of earl' as if it has never enjoyed intoning anything better, and Gene proudly pronounces himself to be the titled gentleman in question. His girl, needless to say, will share the privileges – 'you will be my duchess, duchess of earl'. Rarely has a record rung with such ludicrous conviction, such joy in its own absurdity.

On the 8th the Wilsons and friends' first single 'Surfin'' is released on Candix and credited to the Beach Boys, a name chosen for them by record-distributor Russ Regan. The song is written by Brian Wilson and cousin Mike Love. On the 31st the group play their first concert with the new name at the Ritchie Valens Memorial Concert in Long Beach.

The Beatles meanwhile have agreed to Brian Epstein becoming their manager, and he sets about arranging an audition for them with Decca in London.

USA

1 **Big Bad John**
Jimmy Dean

2 **Runaround Sue**
Dion

3 **Please Mr Postman**
The Marvelettes

4 **Goodbye Cruel World**
James Darren

5 **Fool No. 1**
Brenda Lee

6 **Bristol Stomp**
The Dovells

7 **Heartaches**
The Marcels

8 **Tower of Strength**
Gene McDaniels

9 **Crazy**
Patsy Cline

10 **This Time**
Troy Shondell

UK

1 **Take Good Care of My Baby**
Bobby Vee

2 **His Latest Flame/Little Sister**
Elvis Presley

3 **Big Bad John**
Jimmy Dean

4 **Tower of Strength**
Frankie Vaughan

5 **Moon River**
Danny Williams

6 **The Time Has Come**
Adam Faith

7 **Walkin' Back to Happiness**
Helen Shapiro

8 **Take Five**
Dave Brubeck

9 **The Savage**
The Shadows

10 **I'll Get By**
Shirley Bassey

Gene Chandler, dressed for the part of a duke, earl, or combination of the two.

1962

On the surface 1962 looked much like 1961, but beneath it the pace of change was quickening. Great pop of the traditional sort continued to appear – records like Dion's 'Ruby Baby', Brian Hyland's 'Sealed with a Kiss' and the Everlys' 'Crying in the Rain'. Established performers like Brenda Lee, Roy Orbison and Bobby Vee continued to have hits, and new artists emerged, albeit often with a distinguishing feature that verged on gimmickry. The dance crazes went on.

Artistic self-expression was not uppermost in most singers' minds, and few now wrote their own material. For people like Phil Spector, approaching a peak with the Crystals' early records, and the Beach Boys' Brian Wilson, self-expression had more to do with creating sounds than baring the soul. In the folk clubs of New York, however, it was a different story – here a righteous anger was reaching to be heard. In the R&B-influenced British club scene the reaction was less cerebral, more a matter of energy and exuberance, joy and anger, of freedom for the taking.

Peter, Paul and Mary

Doubtless high on hope, the Beatles travel south on New Year's Day to make an audition tape for Decca. Three days later they are voted best Liverpool group by *Merseybeat* readers, but Decca is not impressed. After sitting on the tape for two months Dick Rowe will reject the group, preferring to sign Brian Poole and the Tremeloes.

Warner Brothers, with rather more foresight, sign up the folk trio Peter, Paul and Mary. They've been brought together the previous year by Albert Grossman as a more will be the first to introduce Grossman's future client Bob Dylan to a wider audience.

In the US 'The Twist' has been re-released on the back of the craze, and goes to #1 again, the first record to hit the top spot twice. Joey Dee and the Starlighters' 'Peppermint Twist' follows it to the top. Sam Cooke releases 'Twistin' the Night Away'.

The Everly Brothers, on weekend leave from the Marines, appear on *The Ed Sullivan Show*, in uniform and with hair shorn to military specifications. They sing their latest single, a Brill Building

USA

1 **The Lion Sleeps Tonight**
The Tokens
2 **The Twist**
Chubby Checker
3 **Run to Him**
Bobby Vee
4 **Peppermint Twist**
Joey Dee & The Starliters
5 **Can't Help Falling in Love**
Elvis Presley
6 **Happy Birthday Sweet Sixteen**
Neil Sedaka
7 **Goodbye Cruel World**
James Darren
8 **Walk on By**
Leroy Van Dyke
9 **When I Fall in Love**
Lettermen
10 **Unchain My Heart**
Ray Charles

UK

1 **Stranger on the Shore**
Acker Bilk
2 **Moon River**
Danny Williams
3 **Let There be Drums**
Sandy Nelson
4 **Johnny Will**
Pat Boone
5 **Tower of Strength**
Frankie Vaughan
6 **Midnight in Moscow**
Kenny Ball
7 **So Long Baby**
Del Shannon
8 **Toy Balloons**
Russ Conway
9 **I'd Never Find Another You**
Billy Fury
10 **My Friend the Sea**
Petula Clark

It's a twisting – not to say twisted – world. Joey Dee and the Starliters perform in the film 'Hey, Let's Twist!'

contemporary version of groups like the Kingston Trio and the Weavers. Their material includes traditional folk, children's songs and protest. In the latter vein they cross-breed by Carole King and Howie Greenfield, 'Crying in the Rain'.

Paul Simon is still trying to be a pop star. After releasing several unsuccessful singles on MGM and Warwick as Jerry Landis, he records 'Motorcycle' for Madison as Tico and the Triumphs. Finally released on Amy, it peaks at #99.

The dance craze finally hits the UK. Both 'The Twist' and 'Let's Twist Again' are re-issued, and the latter wins out, going to #2. Chubby Checker flies in to promote the records and show how it's done on TV. British crooner Frankie Vaughan gets in on the act, reaching the Top Twenty with 'Don't Stop, Twist'.

The UK #1 through most of the month is Cliff Richard's 'The Young Ones'. The movie of the same name, now out on general release, will be the UK's second-highest box office grosser of the year. The soundtrack is already #1 on the album chart. Not surprisingly, Cliff wins the annual *New Musical Express* Top British Male Singer award.

The Shadows, who are also in the movie, release 'Wonderful Land' at the end of the month. One of their most evocative tracks, it will hold the #1 spot for eight weeks in the spring.

In the US Connie Francis releases 'Don't Break the Heart That Loves You'. A typically lachrymose double-tracked ballad, it will be her third and last American #1. In Britain it will only reach #39. The two audiences obviously like different sides of Connie – her two British chart-toppers have only reached #4 and #14 in the US.

The Beach Boys' minor success with 'Surfin'' is not enough to keep Al Jardine away from dentistry college. David Marks comes in on rhythm, Brian Wilson switches to bass, and Dennis Wilson is confirmed as the drummer.

Chuck Berry is finally sentenced to two years' imprisonment in Indiana on the charges brought against him more than two years before – for transporting a girl across a state line for immoral purposes.

USA

1 **Peppermint Twist**
Joey Dee & The Starliters

2 **Can't Help Falling in Love**
Elvis Presley

3 **The Twist**
Chubby Checker

4 **Norman**
Sue Thompson

5 **I Know**
Barbara George

6 **The Wanderer**
Dion

7 **Duke of Earl**
Gene Chandler

8 **Baby It's You**
The Shirelles

9 **Break It to Me Gently**
Brenda Lee

10 **The Lion Sleeps Tonight**
The Tokens

UK

1 **The Young Ones**
Cliff Richard

2 **Rock-A-Hula Baby/Can't Help Falling in Love**
Elvis Presley

3 **Multiplication**
Bobby Darin

4 **Happy Birthday Sweet Sixteen**
Neil Sedaka

5 **Stranger on the Shore**
Acker Bilk

6 **Let's Twist Again**
Chubby Checker

7 **Forget Me Not**
Eden Kane

8 **I'd Never Find Another You**
Billy Fury

9 **Walk on By**
Leroy Vandyke

10 **Let There be Drums**
Sandy Nelson

Cliff Richard, perched on a convenient rock

Bob Dylan's eponymously titled first album is released in the US. It doesn't make the charts, but causes a major stir on the American folk scene. His rough and heartfelt versions of old traditionals like 'The House of the Rising Sun' and 'See That My Grave is Kept Clean' come as a breath of fresh air; the two self-penned songs, when heard in the context of his New York stage appearances, announce the coming of a prodigious talent.

Columbia also issue a single around now. 'Mixed up Confusion' is piano-heavy rockabilly with contemporary-sounding lyrics. It looks forward several albums to the Dylan of *Bringing It All Back Home*.

On the 17th, in the London suburb of Ealing, Blues Incorporated play their first gig. The group is led by guitarist Alexis Korner, and has a policy of letting young devotees sit in on its sessions. Many luminaries of the coming British R&B boom will take up the offer, including Charlie Watts, Mick Jagger and Jack Bruce.

In Manchester the Beatles record four songs for their first radio appearance, on the BBC show *Teenager's Turn*. Versions of Orbison's 'Dream Baby', Chuck Berry's 'Memphis Tennessee' and the Marvelettes' 'Please Mr Postman' – an interesting trio of American influences – are broadcast the following day, but a rendition of their own 'Hello Little Girl' is omitted.

In the US Bruce Channel's 'Hey! Baby' hits the top spot. It's use of bluesy harmonica will find an echo in the Beatles' first single 'Love Me Do'.

USA

1 **Duke of Earl**
Gene Chandler

2 **Hey! Baby**
Bruce Channel

3 **The Wanderer**
Dion

4 **Break It to Me Gently**
Brenda Lee

5 **The Twist**
Chubby Checker

6 **Crying in the Rain**
The Everly Brothers

7 **Norman**
Sue Thompson

8 **Midnight in Moscow**
Kenny Ball

9 **Peppermint Twist**
Joey Dee & The Starliters

10 **Chip Chip**
Gene McDaniels

UK

1 **Rock-A-Hula Baby/Can't Help Falling in Love**
Elvis Presley

2 **Let's Twist Again**
Chubby Checker

3 **March of the Siamese Children**
Kenny Ball

4 **The Young Ones**
Cliff Richard

5 **Tell Me What He Said**
Helen Shapiro

6 **Walk on By**
Leroy Vandyke

7 **Forget Me Not**
Eden Kane

8 **Wimoweh**
Karl Denver

9 **Wonderful Land**
The Shadows

10 **Crying in the Rain**
The Everly Brothers

Blues Incorporated at the Marquee – Cyril Davies on harmonica, Charlie Watts on drums. Inset: Bob Dylan.

Before flying out to begin a seven-week residency at the Star Club in Hamburg, the Beatles have a Fan Club Night at the Cavern. They arrive in the German city on the 11th, to find that ex-group member Stuart Sutcliffe, resident there for the past nine months, has died of a brain haemorrhage the previous evening.

Elvis Presley is #1 in the UK with the double-sided 'Can't Help Falling in Love'/ 'Rock-A-Hula Baby'. Both songs are from the *Blue Hawaii* soundtrack album, which still sits astride the US album chart. His latest film, *Follow That Dream*, a romantic comedy set in the rural South, premières in America on the 11th, and his new single, the lightweight 'Good Luck Charm', becomes his 17th US #1 on the 21st. No one knows it yet, but it's the end of an era – seven and a half years will pass before he has another.

Two leading girl groups are climbing the chart. The Crystals' second single, 'Uptown', a mini-symphony for Spanish Harlem tenement dwellers complete with castanets, is on its way to #13, the Shirelles' 'Soldier Boy' to #1. Both will sell a million.

Saxophone player King Curtis, in the midst of two decades spent gracing other people's records, has his first and biggest moment of solo glory as 'Soul Twist' tops the R&B chart.

At the Ealing Blues Club, friends Mick Jagger and Keith Richards meet pianist Ian Stewart and all-round musician Elmo Lewis, whose real name turns out to be Brian Jones. A group begins to form around the four of them.

USA

1 **Johnny Angel**
Shelley Fabares

2 **Don't Break the Heart That Loves You**
Connie Francis

3 **Good Luck Charm**
Elvis Presley

4 **Slow Twistin'**
Chubby Checker

5 **Dream Baby**
Roy Orbison

6 **Hey! Baby**
Bruce Channel

7 **Midnight in Moscow**
Kenny Ball

8 **Young World**
Rick Nelson

9 **Love Letters**
Ketty Lester

10 **Mashed Potato Time**
Dee Dee Sharp

UK

1 **Wonderful Land**
The Shadows

2 **Tell Me What He Said**
Helen Shapiro

3 **Dream Baby**
Roy Orbison

4 **Rock-A-Hula Baby/Can't Help Falling in Love**
Elvis Presley

5 **Wimoweh**
Karl Denver

6 **Stranger on the Shore**
Acker Bilk

7 **Twistin' The Night Away**
Sam Cooke

8 **Hey Little Girl**
Del Shannon

9 **Hole in the Ground**
Bernard Cribbins

10 **Softly As I Leave You**
Matt Monro

Elvis in the 1960s – no sideburns, no snarl, no class

The Beach Boys' current label Candix goes under, and Wilson Senior, who has assumed a managerial role, takes demos round several companies in search of a new deal. Capitol producer Nick Venet is sufficiently impressed with 'Surfin' Safari' to sign the group up.

The three Isley Brothers have been around rather longer, having moved from Cincinnati to New York in 1957 to record a mixed and largely unsuccessful bag of doo-wop-tinged rock'n'roll. The frenetic and later much-recorded 'Shout', though an R&B hit in 1959, has not crossed over. Now, not so much jumping aboard the bandwagon as using it to pursue their own direction, they release the epochal 'Twist and Shout'. It will reach #17, the first of 11 Top Forty entries spread out across the next 18 years.

In the Memphis studio of Stax Records a group of session musicians (Booker T. Jones, Steve Cropper, Lewis Steinberg and Al Jackson) wind down after backing Billy Lee Riley by recording a couple of impromptu tracks of their own. Jim Stewart, owner of Stax, likes one of the instrumentals enough to release them both as a single under the name Booker T. and the MG's. DJs prefer the 'B' side, 'Green Onions'. By September it's #3 on the US chart.

Having reached #39 earlier in the year with one movie theme (the sulky 'Town without Pity'), Gene Pitney releases another, 'The Man Who Shot Liberty Valance'. This makes better use of his adenoidal tenor and, despite

being completed too late for inclusion in the movie, becomes his first Top Ten record, peaking at #4. In Britain, though, the record makes little impact, and it will be another 18 months before 'Twenty Four Hours From Tulsa' establishes him there.

Gene Pitney on his way to becoming one of the 1960s' rare, male solo success stories

USA

1 **Soldier Boy**
   The Shirelles
2 **Mashed Potato Time**
   Dee Dee Sharp
3 **Johnny Angel**
   Shelley Fabares
4 **Stranger on the Shore**
   Acker Bilk
5 **Good Luck Charm**
   Elvis Presley
6 **Shout**
   Joey Dee & The Starliters
7 **Lover Please**
   Clyde McPhatter
8 **Slow Twistin'**
   Chubby Checker
9 **P.T. 109**
   Jimmy Dean
10 **Twist Twist Senora**
   Gary U.S. Bonds

UK

1 **Wonderful Land**
   The Shadows
2 **Hey Little Girl**
   Del Shannon
3 **Hey! Baby**
   Bruce Channel
4 **Nut Rocker**
   B. Bumble
5 **Dream Baby**
   Roy Orbison
6 **Tell Me What He Said**
   Helen Shapiro
7 **Speak to Me Pretty**
   Brenda Lee
8 **Rock-A-Hula Baby/Can't Help Falling in Love**
   Elvis Presley
9 **Never Goodbye**
   Karl Denver
10 **Stranger on the Shore**
   Acker Bilk

Ray Charles has his third #1 in two years with 'I Can't Stop Loving You', a slow ballad with string and choral accompaniment. The sentimentality of the arrangement can't quite quell the genuine blues feeling in Charles's voice, either on this or the *Modern Sounds in Country* album, just starting a 14-week run atop the album chart.

Bobby Vinton enters the US Top Forty for the first time with 'Roses are Red', also heading for several weeks at #1. His voice has no real feeling to quell, and in any case the song, with its trite sentimental message, doesn't ask for any. It's cute and catchy and nothing else. It's also the first of 30 Top Forty entries for Vinton stretching over more than a decade.

Brian Hyland's 'Sealed with a Kiss' also enters the chart. Though superficially similar to 'Roses are Red' – both are sentimental mini-dramas – the Hyland song has an original arrangement and a vocal performance which perfectly walks the line between pathos and bathos, making it one of the great teen ballads of the era.

In London the newly-formed Island Records releases a first single – Owen Gray's 'Twist Baby'. The company intends to concentrate on importing West Indian music for the British West Indian population, and in the '70s will indeed become the main purveyor of Jamaican reggae. In the meantime it will come to nurture many of the more innovative white British groups – Traffic, Free, Fairport Convention and Jethro Tull among them.

Mike Sarne's novelty record 'Come Outside' follows Elvis's 'Good Luck Charm' to the UK #1 spot. The song also features Wendy Richard, later to become a British TV sitcom and soap star.

After returning from Hamburg the Beatles again travel south for an audition, this time with the head of EMI's Parlophone label, George Martin. He sees and hears something Decca didn't.

Brian Hyland whose two ballad hits this year will provide a definitive statement of teenage romantic angst.

USA

1. **I Can't Stop Loving You**
   Ray Charles
2. **Stranger on the Shore**
   Acker Bilk
3. **Soldier Boy**
   The Shirelles
4. **Lovers Who Wander**
   Dion
5. **Mashed Potato Time**
   Dee Dee Sharp
6. **Everybody Loves Me But You**
   Brenda Lee
7. **Shout! Shout!**
   Ernie Maresca
8. **Old Rivers**
   Walter Brennan
9. **The One Who Really Loves You**
   Mary Wells
10. **The Man Who Shot Liberty Valance**
    Gene Pitney

UK

1. **Good Luck Charm**
   Elvis Presley
2. **I'm Looking out the Window /Do You Want to Dance**
   Cliff Richard
3. **Nut Rocker**
   B. Bumble
4. **Last Night was Made for Love**
   Billy Fury
5. **As You Like It**
   Adam Faith
6. **Come Outside**
   Mike Sarne
7. **Love Letters**
   Ketty Lester
8. **I Don't Know Why**
   Eden Kane
9. **Wonderful Land**
   The Shadows
10. **Ginny Come Lately**
    Brian Hyland

For the Crystals' third single Spector has given them a Goffin-King song – 'He Hit Me (and It Felt Like a Kiss)'. It is almost instantly withdrawn when DJs take exception to the lyric, but luck is with Spector – a better song is offered to him by Gene Pitney.

Spector is in Los Angeles, the Crystals in New York, and the lack of exclusive rights to the song means they have to act quickly, but no matter. The artists are the last thing Spector needs. 'He's a Rebel' is recorded with Darlene Love singing lead, and session vocalists in support. Also present, among others, are Jack Nitzsche (a young arranger who will later work with Neil Young and other LA luminaries, besides developing a career in movie music), Sonny Bono (of future Sonny and Cher fame, on percussion) and Hal Blaine (on drums).

Between them they conjure up the 'sound'. Not yet the fabled 'wall of sound', but Spector is getting close. 'He's a Rebel' is an opera on the move, rumbling, soaring, dancing. Tenement Wagner.

Meanwhile, Buddy Holly's influence is obviously still being felt. The Crickets' 'Don't Ever Change' (another Goffin-King song) is on its way to #5 in the British chart, and Tommy Roe's 'Sheila', just released in the States, seems as near-perfect a re-run of 'Peggy Sue' as the copyright laws allow. It will reach #1 in the US, #3 in the UK.

At the Marquee Club in London the newly named Rolling Stones – comprising Jagger, Richards, Jones, Ian Stewart, bassist Dick Taylor and drummer Mick Avory – make their stage debut.

Joe Brown

USA

1 **The Stripper**
David Rose

2 **Roses Are Red**
Bobby Vinton

3 **I Can't Stop Loving You**
Ray Charles

4 **Palisades Park**
Freddy Cannon

5 **It Keeps Right on A-Hurtin'**
Johnny Tillotson

6 **Al Di La**
Emilio Pericoli

7 **Wolverton Mountain**
Claude King

8 **Snap Your Fingers**
Joe Henderson

9 **Johnny Get Angry**
Joanie Sommers

10 **Playboy**
The Marvelettes

UK

1 **Come Outside**
Mike Sarne

2 **A Picture of You**
Joe Brown

3 **Good Luck Charm**
Elvis Presley

4 **I Can't Stop Loving You**
Ray Charles

5 **Ginny Come Lately**
Brian Hyland

6 **I'm Looking out the Window /Do You Want to Dance**
Cliff Richard

7 **Green Leaves of Summer**
Kenny Ball & his Jazzmen

8 **Ain't That Funny**
Jimmy Justice

9 **Stranger on the Shore**
Acker Bilk

10 **Sharing You**
Bobby Vee

On the 18th Richard Starkey, alias Ringo Starr, makes his debut as a Beatle at a Cavern gig, replacing Pete Best at the instigation of either George Martin, Brian Epstein or the other Beatles, depending on who you want to believe.

minor British hit until, over a quarter of a century later, the movie *Blue Velvet* sends his 1963 American hit of that name up the UK chart.

The Four Seasons' 'Sherry' enters the US chart at #91, on its way to #1. An ideal vehicle for lead singer Frankie Valli's

including their other three chart-toppers – 'Big Girls Don't Cry', 'Walk like a Man' and their classic song 'Rag Doll'.

'Sherry' is something of a novelty record. So is the UK #1, Frank Ifield's 'I Remember You', a routine

their babysitter, Little Eva, but any reasonable voice could have handled it. Like 'Sherry' and 'I Remember You' it's hardly a song which calls for artistic self-expression. That, in the last years of the pre-Beatles/Dylan era, is becoming increasingly a prerogative granted only to writers and producers.

USA

1 **Roses Are Red**
Bobby Vinton

2 **Breaking up is Hard to Do**
Neil Sedaka

3 **Sealed with a Kiss**
Brian Hyland

4 **The Wah-Watusi**
The Orlons

5 **Ahab the Arab**
Ray Stevens

6 **Speedy Gonzales**
Pat Boone

7 **I Can't Stop Loving You**
Ray Charles

8 **Loco-Motion**
Little Eva

9 **The Stripper**
David Rose

10 **Theme from Doctor Kildare**
Richard Chamberlain

UK

1 **I Remember You**
Frank Ifield

2 **I Can't Stop Loving You**
Ray Charles

3 **Speedy Gonzales**
Pat Boone

4 **A Picture of You**
Joe Brown

5 **Don't Ever Change**
The Crickets

6 **Come Outside**
Mike Sarne

7 **Here Comes That Feeling**
Brenda Lee

8 **Little Miss Lonely**
Helen Shapiro

9 **English Country Garden**
Jimmy Rodgers

10 **Right, Said Fred**
Bernard Cribbins

On the British chart Ronnie Carroll's cover version of 'Roses are Red' outsells Bobby Vinton's original, reaching #3 to the other's #15. Despite continuing US success, Vinton will manage only one more

distinctive falsetto, it has been written by the group's latest recruit, ex-Royal Teen Bob Gaudio. He and producer Bob Crewe will write many of the Four Seasons' biggest hits over the next few years,

singalong ballad made memorable only by periodic yodelling. 'The Loco-Motion', US #1 at the month's end, is a dance record. It has been written by Carole King and Gerry Goffin and donated to

The Beatles' early days – the centre shot includes Pete Best (centre left)

Peter, Paul and Mary's second single is a spirited rendition of Pete Seeger's 'If I Had a Hammer'. The song, with its ringing demand for 'justice all over this land', seems perfectly attuned to the righteous naivety of the Kennedy era. It climbs the chart as the Cuban Missile Crisis unfolds, providing musical accompaniment to a world suddenly in need of reassurance.

Bob Dylan appears at a Carnegie Hall 'Hootenanny' and performs five numbers, including one which will cause him trouble the following year, 'John Birch Society Talking Blues'.

Out on the West Coast everyone's too busy watching the waves to worry about such matters. The Beach Boys'

USA

1 **Sheila**
Tommy Roe

2 **You Don't Know Me**
Ray Charles

3 **Loco-Motion**
Little Eva

4 **Ramblin' Rose**
Nat 'King' Cole

5 **She's Not You**
Elvis Presley

6 **Breaking up is Hard to Do**
Neil Sedaka

7 **Party Lights**
Claudine Clark

8 **Things**
Bobby Darin

9 **Teen Age Idol**
Rick Nelson

10 **Vacation**
Connie Francis

'Surfin' Safari' is released on Capitol, and will give them their first Top Twenty entry, rising to #14. With its Chuck

UK

1 **I Remember You**
Frank Ifield

2 **Speedy Gonzales**
Pat Boone

3 **Things**
Bobby Darin

4 **Guitar Tango**
The Shadows

5 **Sealed with a Kiss**
Brian Hyland

6 **Roses are Red**
Ronnie Carroll

7 **Once upon a Dream**
Billy Fury

8 **Breaking up is Hard to Do**
Neil Sedaka

9 **I Can't Stop Loving You**
Ray Charles

10 **Vacation**
Connie Francis

Berry beat, overlapping harmonies and celebration of a world where bronzed beauties of both sexes have

nothing to do but wax their surfboards, it sets the Wilsons' flag in the Californian sand.

On a more serious – not to say grave – note, Bobby 'Boris' Pickett and the Crypt Kickers release the novelty 'Monster Mash'. A harmless invitation to dance with pulp heroes like Dracula and Frankenstein, it will reach #1 in October. In Britain the BBC manages, not for the first time, to make a collective fool of itself by banning the record. The corruption of the nation's youth is postponed until the record's re-release after a safe 11 years in 1973.

On the 11th, in EMI's Abbey Road studio, George Martin supervises the recording of the first Beatles single, 'Love Me Do'/'PS I Love You'. Both songs are Lennon-McCartney compositions.

The Beach Boys with surfboard and woody

For several years now James Brown has been criss-crossing America with a live show that seems to defy description. Using uptempo numbers as a setting for wonderfully choreographed dance spectaculars, slow-burning ballads as a basis for cathartic sermonizing, and the whole as an excuse for gorgeous costumes, he has broken box office records right across black America. On the 24th the show is recorded *Live at the Apollo Theater*, and the subsequent album sells an unprecedented (for an R&B artist) million copies, besides gaining a reputation as one of the finest concert albums ever released.

Motown's momentum is also gathering pace. Twelve-year-old musical prodigy Steveland Morris Judkins releases his first single, 'Thank You for Loving Me All The Way', under the name Little Stevie Wonder. He's already on tour at the time of release with other label artists the Miracles, Mary Wells, Marvin Gaye and the Supremes.

The Beatles sign a five-year contract with Brian Epstein, and on the 5th 'Love Me Do' is released in the UK (it will not be released in the US until 1964). A week later it enters the charts at #49, and will eventually peak at #17. On the 12th the group appears at Liverpool's New Brighton Tower, as one of the supporting acts for Little Richard, on his comeback tour. Paul McCartney asks the great man to give him some singing tips.

Stardom seems to be taking its toll on some of the older stars. During rehearsals for a British tour Don Everly collapses on stage at London's Prince of Wales theatre. The official explanation is nervous exhaustion. Phil continues the tour alone.

USA

1 **Sherry**
Four Seasons

2 **Monster Mash**
Bobby (Boris) Pickett
and The Crypt Kickers

3 **Ramblin' Rose**
Nat 'King' Cole

4 **Let's Dance**
Chris Montez

5 **Green Onions**
Booker T & The MG's

6 **Patches**
Dickey Lee

7 **Venus in Blue Jeans**
Jimmy Clanton

8 **I Remember You**
Frank Ifield

9 **Alley Cat**
Bent Fabric

10 **You Beat Me to the Punch**
Mary Wells

UK

1 **Telstar**
The Tornadoes

2 **She's Not for You**
Elvis Presley

3 **It'll be Me**
Cliff Richard

4 **Sheila**
Tommy Roe

5 **Loco-Motion**
Little Eva

6 **It Might As Well Rain Until September**
Carole King

7 **Sealed with a Kiss**
Brian Hyland

8 **I Remember You**
Frank Ifield

9 **You Don't Know Me**
Ray Charles

10 **Don't That Beat All**
Adam Faith

Stars of the coming decade – (left) Marvin Gaye and (right) James Brown

Motown releases the Miracles' sinuous 'You've Really Got a Hold on Me'. It will be their first Top Ten hit since 'Shop Around' two years before, and the first of many successful Motown records both written and produced by the group's lead singer Smokey Robinson.

Together again, Lee Hazlewood and Duane Eddy come up with one more massive hit for the guitarist by dressing up the familiar twangy guitar line with a female chorus. 'Dance with the Guitar Man' will reach #4 in the UK, #12 in the US.

Seventeen-year-old Dee Dee Sharp has done as well out of the dance craze as anyone save Chubby Checker. Having started out as a Philadelphia session singer at the age of 15, providing back-up vocals on, among others, Checker's own 'Slow Twistin'', she's already had two solo hits in 1962 with the million-selling 'Mashed Potato Time' and its sequel 'Gravy (For My Mashed Potatoes)'. Her 'Ride!', which is released this month, will also go gold.

Brenda Lee continues to churn out high-quality singles in a variety of styles. After the rocking 'Here Comes That Feeling' and the bluesy 'Heart in Hand' comes the lush ballad 'All Alone Am I'. Her seventeenth Top Forty entry, it will eventually reach #3.

Peter, Paul and Mary is #1 on the album chart for the whole month, just as Judy Garland's *Judy at Carnegie Hall* had been the previous November. These two albums, though separated by only 12 months, have been made by and for different generations.

Smokey Robinson (left) and the Miracles

USA

1 **He's a Rebel**
The Crystals

2 **Only Love Can Break a Heart**
Gene Pitney

3 **Do You Love Me**
Contours

4 **Monster Mash**
Bobby (Boris) Pickett
and The Crypt Kickers

5 **All Alone Am I**
Brenda Lee

6 **Big Girls Don't Cry**
Four Seasons

7 **Gina**
Johnny Mathis

8 **Limbo Rock**
Chubby Checker

9 **Next Door to an Angel**
Neil Sedaka

10 **Return to Sender**
Elvis Presley

UK

1 **Telstar**
The Tornadoes

2 **Let's Dance**
Chris Montez

3 **Loco-Motion**
Little Eva

4 **Venus in Blue Jeans**
Mark Wynter

5 **Lovesick Blues**
Frank Ifield

6 **It Might As Well Rain Until September**
Carole King

7 **Ramblin' Rose**
Nat 'King' Cole

8 **Swiss Maid**
Del Shannon

9 **Sheila**
Tommy Roe

10 **She's Not You**
Elvis Presley

The year ends, bizarrely, with Billy Fury's backing group the Tornadoes becoming the first British group to top the US chart. 'Telstar' is a whooshing, humming, whirring instrumental, concocted by English producer Joe Meek as a tribute to the telecommunications satellite launched the previous summer. It has already spent five weeks atop the British chart.

Bobby Vee's 'The Night Has a Thousand Eyes' enters the US charts. Though a huge success, going to #3 on both sides of the Atlantic, the record shows that even the class of '61 is suffering the strains of keeping up with musical changes. The stark simplicity of the earlier arrangements is gone, and Vee's voice is almost overwhelmed by the production.

The Drifters, by contrast, are about to find a new lease of life after two years of only middling chart success. 'Up on the Roof' is the first of their three Top Ten 'location' hits; 'On Broadway' and 'Under the Boardwalk' will follow in succeeding years.

After a succession of interminable delays, Alan Freed finally goes on trial on payola charges. He admits that on two specific dates in 1958 he had been paid a total of $2,700 for playing certain records on his New York radio show. Freed is fined $300 and given six months' probation.

In Britain the Springfields' 'Island of Dreams' is released on Philips. Both it and the next single, 'Say I Won't Be There', will reach #5, but the group, voted best in the UK by *New Musical Express* readers the previous year, will not survive 1963.

The Beatles are doing their last stint in Hamburg. The Stones, impressed by his amplifier, hire Bill Wyman as their bassist.

USA

1 **Big Girls Don't Cry**
The Four Seasons

2 **Return to Sender**
Elvis Presley

3 **Bobby's Girl**
Marcie Blane

4 **Don't Hang Up**
The Orlons

5 **Ride!**
Dee Dee Sharp

6 **The Lonely Bull**
Tijuana Brass

7 **Telstar**
The Tornados

8 **Limbo Rock**
Chubby Checker

9 **All Alone Am I**
Brenda Lee

10 **Release Me**
Little Esther

UK

1 **Lovesick Blues**
Frank Ifield

2 **Swiss Maid**
Del Shannon

3 **Bobby's Girl**
Susan Maughan

4 **Let's Dance**
Chris Montez

5 **Devil Woman**
Marty Robbins

6 **Dance with the Guitar Man**
Duane Eddy

7 **Venus in Blue Jeans**
Mark Wynter

8 **Sun Arise**
Rolf Harris

9 **Telstar**
The Tornadoes

10 **Loco-Motion**
Little Eva

Bobby Vee, nearing the end of his run of chart success, stakes everything on the right shirt.

1963

This was the year Britain and the US took temporary leave of each other's company. In America 1963 was much like 1962 except more so. Spector moved from Crystals to Ronettes, the Beach Boys from surfboards to hot rods. Motown's inventiveness continued to blossom, and the folk movement moved towards the mainstream with TV's *Hootenanny* and Peter, Paul and Mary's successful popularization of Dylan's new songs. Only a new unifying force was lacking.

It surfaced in Britain, where a host of new groups emerged from the clubs of London and the cities of the north. Most were influenced by American R&B and Everly-style harmony singing; all seemed to overflow with the energy and enthusiasm so lacking in most contemporary pop.

For the moment none could compare with the Beatles, who used 1963 to sweep aside all opposition with a completeness not seen since Elvis's conquest of America seven years before. Like most of rock'n'roll's founding fathers, the Beatles wrote great songs and made the great songs of others their own, synthesizing styles with an effortless joy and utter indifference to conventional wisdom.

The Beatles

112

As it stands today, there's virtually no difference between rock'n'roll, pop and rhythm and blues. The music has completely overlapped.' So Leonard Chess, co-founder of the famous record company, tells *Billboard* on the fifth day of the new year. It's a statement that begs a lot of questions, particularly at the beginning of a year which will see an enormous schism open up between the British and American music scenes.

Reading Chess's assertion Bobby Bland might be wondering why his R&B chart-topping 'That's the Way Love is' can only manage #33 on the pop chart. Bob Dylan, in London to record a TV play (in which he plays a hobo and sings 'Blowin' in the Wind'), might wonder how the folk movement fits into it all.

True, it's easier to cross the boundaries between musics,

USA

1. **Telstar**
   The Tornadoes
2. **Go away Little Girl**
   Steve Lawrence
3. **Limbo Rock**
   Chubby Checker
4. **Bobby's Girl**
   Marcie Blane
5. **Big Girls Don't Cry**
   The Four Seasons
6. **Hotel Happiness**
   Brook Benton
7. **Pepino the Italian Mouse**
   Lou Monte
8. **Return to Sender**
   Elvis Presley
9. **Zip-A-Dee-Doo-Dah**
   Bob B. Soxx
   & The Blue Jeans
10. **Tell Him**
    The Exciters

Chubby Checker and (inset)
Bobby 'Blue' Bland

but the different musical forms are still there. The original rock'n'roll synthesis is now yesterday's news, and its popularized mutation (pop for short) is growing stale, increasingly reliant on gimmick, traditional virtues (original melody, a good voice) and innovative production to differentiate its product.

UK

1. **The Next Time/Bachelor Boy**
   Cliff Richard
2. **Return to Sender**
   Elvis Presley
3. **Lovesick Blues**
   Frank Ifield
4. **Sun Arise**
   Rolf Harris
5. **Dance with the Guitar Man**
   Duane Eddy
6. **Bobby's Girl**
   Susan Maughan
7. **Dance On!**
   The Shadows
8. **It Only Took a Minute**
   Joe Brown
9. **Telstar**
   The Tornadoes
10. **Let's Dance**
    Chris Montez

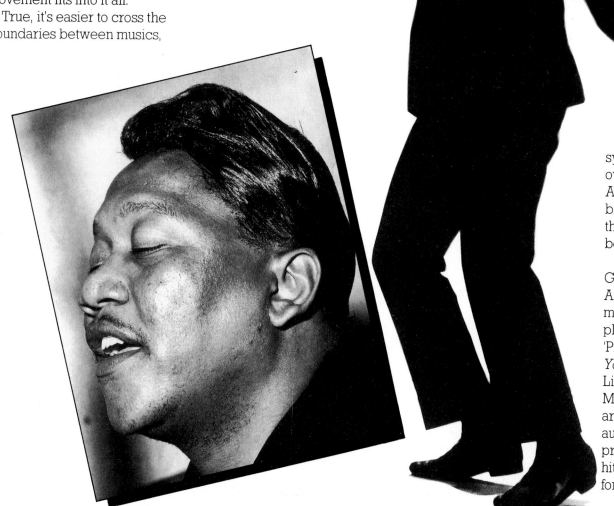

It is outside this central synthesis, outside the overlapping realms of American music, in the folk, black and British club scenes, that the immediate future can be seen and heard.

On the 11th the Whiskey-a-Go-Go club opens in Los Angeles, and the Beatles make their British TV debut, playing their new single 'Please Please Me' on *Thank Your Lucky Stars*. At Liverpool's Cavern Club, Manchester group the Hollies are good enough to earn an audition from a watching EMI producer. A young Janis Joplin hitch-hikes to San Francisco for the first time.

113

As always, the charts are the last place to look for new musical trends. At #1 in the US a superior ballad (Steve Lawrence's 'Go away Little Girl') is succeeded by a folky novelty number (The Rooftop Singers' 'Walk Right In'), and that by a slice of gloriously anachronistic teeny-pop (Paul and Paula's 'Hey Paula').

In the UK five hits by Cliff, The Shadows and ex-Shadows – 'The Next Time', 'Dance On', 'Diamonds', 'Summer Holiday' and 'Foot Tapper' – follow each other to #1 between early January and early April. Only Frank Ifield's 'The Wayward Wind' manages to interrupt this procession, for a mere three weeks. 'Please Please Me' reaches #2 behind him.

The Beatles' single is released in the US on Vee Jay, but no one notices. The boys are on their first British tour, supporting Helen Shapiro. On the 11th they break off to record the remaining songs for the *Please Please Me* album in the Abbey Road studio. It takes them 12 hours.

In the US the Chiffons' 'He's So Fine', which will later be successfully claimed as the blueprint for George Harrison's 'My Sweet Lord', is released on Laurie. It will go to #1 on both pop and R&B charts, as will one of the month's new chart entries, Ruby and the Romantics' 'Our Day Will Come'. Two chart climbers are Dion and Dionne (Warwick) – the former with the sexy Leiber and Stoller number 'Ruby Baby', the latter making her debut with 'Don't Make Me Over', which has been written and produced by rising stars Burt Bacharach and Hal David.

Dionne Warwick, beginning a string of hits with the Bacharach-David song 'Don't Make Me Over'

USA

1 **Walk Right In**
Rooftop Singers

2 **Hey Paula**
Paul and Paula

3 **The Night Has a Thousand Eyes**
Bobby Vee

4 **Go Away Little Girl**
Steve Lawrence

5 **Loop De Loop**
Johnny Thunder

6 **It's Up to You**
Rick Nelson

7 **Up on the Roof**
The Drifters

8 **Tell Him**
The Exciters

9 **Two Lovers**
Mary Wells

10 **My Dad**
Paul Petersen

UK

1 **Diamonds**
Jet Harris and Tony Meehan

2 **The Next Time/Bachelor Boy**
Cliff Richard

3 **Like I Do**
Maureen Evans

4 **Dance On!**
The Shadows

5 **Globe-Trotter**
The Tornadoes

6 **Don't You Think It's Time**
Mike Berry & The Outlaws

7 **Little Town Flirt**
Del Shannon

8 **Return to Sender**
Elvis Presley

9 **Wayward Wind**
Frank Ifield

10 **Some Kinda Fun**
Chris Montez

Otis Redding. Inset: Bobby Darin

In recognition of folk's growing popularity ABC-TV has a new showcase – *Hootenanny* – due to begin in April. The lack of any parallel recognition of the reasons for this trend becomes somewhat obvious when ABC decide to ban Pete Seeger and the Weavers on political grounds. Joan Baez immediately says she won't appear on the programme. Fifty folk singers gather in Greenwich Village to discuss action, perhaps inspired by the new American #1, the Four Seasons' 'Walk Like a Man'.

On the British R&B scene sax and keyboard player Graham Bond leaves Blues Incorporated to start his own band, the Graham Bond Organisation, along with future Cream stalwarts Jack Bruce and Ginger Baker. Another recently formed group with a jazz background, Manfred Mann, make their first major public appearance at the Marquee Club.

Canadian rocker Ronnie Hawkins, who has been traversing the continent for several years with his backing group the Hawks (later the Band), records a version of Bo Diddley's 'Who Do You Love?'. It fails to sell, but will be much admired in later years, particularly for the astonishingly precocious guitar solo by young Robbie Robertson. One critic will call the record 'possibly the most menacing piece of rock'n'roll ever made'.

On the 5th 'heartbreak ballad' singer Patsy Cline, undisputed queen of country music, is killed in an air crash. On the 23rd Otis Redding, who will suffer a similar fate, makes his R&B chart debut with 'These Arms of Mine'.

The Beatles are touring again, topping the bill after the first night's crowds make it plain it's not Chris Montez and Tommy Roe they've come to see. On the 22nd their debut album *Please Please Me* is released. It will take only three weeks to reach #1 on the album chart. The pace of change, at least in Britain, is quickening.

USA

1 **Walk Like a Man**
The Four Seasons

2 **Ruby Baby**
Dion

3 **Hey Paula**
Paul and Paula

4 **Rhythm of the Rain**
The Cascades

5 **Walk Right In**
Rooftop Singers

6 **You're the Reason I'm Living**
Bobby Darin

7 **Blame It on the Bossa Nova**
Eydie Gorme

8 **From a Jack to a King**
Ned Miller

9 **Wild Weekend**
The Rebels

10 **What Will My Mary Say**
Johnny Mathis

UK

1 **Wayward Wind**
Frank Ifield

2 **Please Please Me**
The Beatles

3 **The Night Has a Thousand Eyes**
Bobby Vee

4 **Diamonds**
Jet Harris and Tony Meehan

5 **Loop-De-Loop**
Frankie Vaughan

6 **That's What Love Will Do**
Joe Brown

7 **Summer Holiday**
Cliff Richard & The Shadows

8 **Little Town Flirt**
Del Shannon

9 **Island of Dreams**
The Springfields

10 **Suki Yaki**
Kenny Ball & his Jazzmen

The first Liverpool group hits #1 in Britain, but it's not the Beatles. Brian Epstein's second signings, Gerry and the Pacemakers, have also been signed by Parlophone and produced by George Martin. 'How Do You Do It?' is typical Merseybeat of the time – long on brash energy and rhythm, short on smooth-sounding production. Like the Beatles, the group have a repertoire full of classic American rock'n'roll and R&B standards; unlike them, they write no great songs of their own.

The Beatles' first #1 will be 'From Me to You'. Released on the 11th, it will reach the top on 4 May, by which time the foursome will be headlining their first tour, supported by Roy Orbison and Gerry and the Pacemakers. The record will remain at #1 for seven weeks.

The Rolling Stones now have a regular gig at the Crawdaddy Club in Richmond, and the 28th finds Andrew Loog Oldham, 19-year-old music business publicist, in the audience. The next day he signs them to his management.

The sense of changing times is making it hard for established acts. The Everly Brothers release 'So It Always will Be', a record not noticeably inferior in quality to the previous year's 'Crying in the Rain'. It doesn't even make the Top Hundred in the US, and only reaches #23 in Britain.

Roy Orbison is still in there fighting. 'In Dreams', his definitive statement of the human condition as endless pathos, will reach #7 in the US, #6 in the UK.

Gerry and the Pacemakers – perhaps checking the number of zeros on their advance

USA

1 **He's So Fine**
The Chiffons

2 **Our Day Will Come**
Ruby and The Romantics

3 **The End of the World**
Skeeter Davis

4 **South Street**
The Orlons

5 **Can't Get Used to Losing You**
Andy Williams

6 **Baby Workout**
Jackie Wilson

7 **In Dreams**
Roy Orbison

8 **You're the Reason I'm Living**
Bobby Darin

9 **Rhythm of the Rain**
The Cascades

10 **Young Lovers**
Paul and Paula

UK

1 **How Do You Do It?**
Gerry & The Pacemakers

2 **From a Jack to a King**
Ned Miller

3 **Summer Holiday**
Cliff Richard & The Shadows

4 **Foot Tapper**
The Shadows

5 **Like I've Never Been Gone**
Billy Fury

6 **Say Wonderful Things**
Ronnie Carroll

7 **Rhythm of the Rain**
The Cascades

8 **Charmaine**
The Bachelors

9 **Brown Eyed Handsome Man**
Buddy Holly

10 **That's What Love Will Do**
Joe Brown

Despite being boycotted by most of America's leading exponents, ABC-TV's folk music programme *Hootenanny* has started up the previous month. That ABC are not alone in their attitudes becomes apparent on the 12th, when CBS censors tell Bob Dylan, during the dress rehearsal, that he can't perform 'John Birch Society Talking Blues' on *The Ed Sullivan Show*. The song may be libellous, they say. Dylan walks out.

Five days later he gets rave reviews for his performance at the first Monterey Folk Festival. Peter, Paul and Mary, Pete Seeger and the Weavers, Joan Baez, and others espousing ABC's 'radical causes' also appear. It's the first meeting between Dylan and Baez, who will go on to develop an important professional (and personal) relationship.

Meanwhile Dylan's second album, *The Freewheelin' Bob Dylan*, is released to critical acclaim. This time nearly all the songs are self-penned; they include both protest anthems and songs tackling romantic themes with a rare directness.

On the 21st Little Stevie Wonder records his first album, *The Twelve-Year-Old Genius*, live in Detroit. He's been 13 for eight days, but who cares? A track from the album, 'Fingertips Part 2', will be his first hit, reaching #1 on both pop and R&B charts.

The two US #1s of the month are Little Peggy March's 'I Will Follow Him' and Jimmy Soul's 'If You Wanna Be Happy'. More memorable, and rising fast, is Lesley Gore's 'It's My Party', a

Little Stevie Wonder, holding the famous harmonica, takes the record-buying world by storm.

song which raises petulance to an art form. Later in the year Gore will provide her own answer record, 'Judy's Turn to Cry', and early in 1964 a classic slice of proto-feminist pop, 'You Don't Own Me.'

In Chicago blues guitarist Elmore James dies of a coronary, aged 45. His characteristic style of heavily-amplified slide guitar-playing will be a major influence on British groups like the original Fleetwood Mac and John Mayall's Bluesbreakers.

USA

1. **I Will Follow Him**
   Little Peggy March
2. **Can't Get Used to Losing You**
   Andy Williams
3. **Puff**
   Peter, Paul and Mary
4. **Pipline**
   The Chantays
5. **He's So Fine**
   The Chiffons
6. **If You Wanna be Happy**
   Jimmy Soul
7. **Don't Say Nothin' Bad About My Baby**
   The Cookies
8. **Surfin' U.S.A.**
   Beach Boys
9. **On Broadway**
   The Drifters
10. **Watermelon Man**
    Mongo Santamaria

UK

1. **From Me to You**
   The Beatles
2. **How Do You Do It?**
   Gerry & The Pacemakers
3. **From a Jack to a King**
   Ned Miller
4. **Nobody's Darlin' But Mine**
   Frank Ifield
5. **Say I Won't Be There**
   The Springfields
6. **Can't Get Used to Losing You**
   Andy Williams
7. **In Dreams**
   Roy Orbison
8. **Rhythm of the Rain**
   The Cascades
9. **Brown Eyed Handsome Man**
   Buddy Holly
10. **Foot Tapper**
    The Shadows

Andrew Loog Oldham has wasted no time with his new protégés. Before their signatures are dry on the contract he's had the Rolling Stones auditioning for Decca's Beatle-rejector Dick Rowe, and Rowe has had the sense not to make another mistake of similar proportions.

On the 7th the band make their first TV appearance and release their first single. Each has something missing. Pianist Ian Stewart, who looks as straight as the others don't, has been removed from the visual frame by Oldham, and henceforth will be the invisible sixth Stone. Chuck Berry's 'Come On' has lost the phrase 'some stupid jerk', just in case the BBC find it objectionable. 'Some stupid guy' has been substituted.

On the British chart the Beatles are still at #1; their composition 'Do You Want to Know a Secret?' for fellow Merseysiders Billy J. Kramer and the Dakotas is at #2. The Searchers' first single, 'Sweets

USA

1 **It's My Party**
Lesley Gore

2 **Sukiyaki**
Kyu Sakamoto

3 **Da Doo Ron Ron**
The Crystals

4 **I Love You Because**
Al Martino

5 **You Can't Sit Down**
The Dovells

6 **Two Faces Have I**
Lou Christie

7 **If You Wanna Be Happy**
Jimmy Soul

8 **Still**
Bill Anderson

9 **Those Lazy-Hazy-Crazy Days of Summer**
Nat 'King' Cole

10 **Surfin' U.S.A.**
Beach Boys

UK

1 **From Me to You**
The Beatles

2 **Do You Want to Know a Secret?**
Billy J. Kramer
& The Dakotas

3 **Scarlett O'Hara**
Jet Harris and Tony Meehan

4 **Lucky Lips**
Cliff Richard

5 **Can't Get Used To Losing You**
Andy Williams

6 **Two Kinds of Teardrops**
Del Shannon

7 **When Will You Say I Love You?**
Billy Fury

8 **In Dreams**
Roy Orbison

9 **Young Lovers**
Paul and Paula

10 **Deck of Cards**
Wink Martindale

for My Sweet', is released, and Gerry and the Pacemakers' second, 'I Like It', enters the chart – both will

reach #1. Brian Epstein signs up the Fourmost, and in Liverpool itself would-be agents and managers scour the clubs and streets for any remaining groups still hidden in the brickwork.

In the US there is still no reaction. The Beatles are in the charts for the first time, but only as composers – Del Shannon is gaining some recompense for all those years of British cover versions of American hits, taking 'From Me to You' to #77.

Motown is supplying most of what dynamism there is in the American scene. On the 15th Marvin Gaye's 'Pride and Joy' enters the charts, on the way to becoming his first Top Ten hit.

It's as easy as falling off a wall – the 'infant' Rolling Stones.

Young Bob Zimmerman – better known as Bob Dylan – in the studio. Inset: the Beach Boys

USA

1 **Easier Said Than Done**
Essex

2 **Sukiyaki**
Kyu Sakamoto

3 **Blue on Blue**
Bobby Vinton

4 **Hello Stranger**
Barbara Lewis

5 **It's My Party**
Lesley Gore

6 **One Fine Day**
The Chiffons

7 **Surf City**
Jan & Dean

8 **Memphis**
Lonnie Mack

9 **So Much in Love**
Tymes

10 **Tie Me Kangaroo Down Sport**
Rolf Harris

UK

1 **I Like It**
Gerry & The Pacemakers

2 **Atlantis**
The Shadows

3 **Confessin'**
Frank Ifield

4 **If You Gotta Make a Fool of Somebody**
Freddie & The Dreamers

5 **Deck of Cards**
Wink Martindale

6 **Take These Chains from My Heart**
Ray Charles

7 **Bo Diddley**
Buddy Holly

8 **From Me to You**
The Beatles

9 **Welcome to My World**
Jim Reeves

10 **Falling**
Roy Orbison

The search for new thrills goes on. By night new releases from the Miracles and Major Lance ('Mickey's Monkey' and 'Monkey Time') lead fashionably simian gyrations on the dance floor. By day young Americans hum along to songs about kids loading up the woody with their boards and other Californian esoterica. 'Surfer Girl' is about to become the Beach Boys' third surfing hit; Jan and Dean, last seen making 'Jennie Lee' in a garage, are establishing themselves as the other authority on beach life. 'Surf City', with its joyous announcement of pre-feminist paradise ('two girls for every boy'), goes all the way to #1.

In London John Mayall's Bluesbreakers make their club debut. Over the next few years the band will serve as a launching pad for rock-blues guitarists Eric Clapton, Peter Green and Mick Taylor.

On the 29th the Newport Folk Festival opens – for the first time since 1959 – in Newport, Rhode Island. The stars are, in Pete Seeger's phrase, 'Woody's children' – the young, the angry, the committed: Baez, Tom Paxton, Phil Ochs, Peter, Paul and Mary, Ramblin' Jack Elliott, and, above all, Dylan.

The intertwining of attitudes and music which this group of artists represents has still to reach the charts and minds of mainstream America, but that moment is not far off. Early in July Peter, Paul and Mary's version of 'Blowin' in the Wind' is released. By the end of August it will have reached #2 on the pop chart, and sold a million.

Almost overnight radicalism will spell dollars. By fall the number of promoters scouring Greenwich Village for folk singers will match that scouring Liverpool for groups.

119

USA

1 **So Much in Love**
Tymes

2 **Fingertips**
Little Stevie Wonder

3 **Surf City**
Jan and Dean

4 **Devil in Disguise**
Elvis Presley

5 **Wipe Out**
Surfaris

6 **Blowin' in the Wind**
Peter, Paul and Mary

7 **Easier Said Than Done**
Essex

8 **Judy's Turn to Cry**
Lesley Gore

9 **Tie Me Kangaroo Down Sport**
Rolf Harris

10 **Just One Look**
Doris Troy

UK

1 **Devil in Disguise**
Elvis Presley

2 **Confessin'**
Frank Ifield

3 **Sweets for My Sweet**
The Searchers

4 **Twist and Shout**
Brian Poole & The Tremeloes

5 **Da Doo Ron Ron**
The Crystals

6 **I Like It**
Gerry & The Pacemakers

7 **Atlantis**
The Shadows

8 **Suki Yaki**
Kyu Sakamoto

9 **Welcome to My World**
Jim Reeves

10 **It's My Party**
Lesley Gore

Motown goes from strength to strength on the charts. Marvin Gaye's 'Pride and Joy' is on the way down, the Miracles' 'Mickey's Monkey' on the way up. Martha and the Vandellas' new release 'Heat Wave' will go to #4. Most gratifying of all, on the 24th Little Stevie Wonder becomes the first artist ever to top the pop, R&B and album charts in the same week.

The other major source of American pop innovation, Phil Spector, is now at his peak. The Crystals' 'Da Doo Ron Ron' has just dropped out of the chart: the follow-up 'Then He Kissed Me' is about to enter. The Ronettes' 'Be My Baby', featuring lead vocal by Spector's future wife, Ronnie, will be released in September. All three are 'wall of sound' classics, with multiple instrumentation (four pianos, for example) and extensive overdubbing, everything deepened by echo, layer piled on layer to build mini-cathedrals of sound.

In Britain the Beatles perform at the Cavern for the last time on the 3rd. Six days later the ground-breaking TV show *Ready Steady Go* begins. Over the next few years it will offer a national stage for the British group boom, much as *American Bandstand* did for rock'n'roll's mutation into pop.

On the 28th Martin Luther King delivers his 'I Have a Dream' speech from the steps of the Lincoln Memorial in Washington to a huge gathering of civil rights protesters, Bob Dylan and Joan Baez among them.

The '60s start here – Peter, Paul and Mary on 'Ready Steady Go'

USA

1 **My Boyfriend's Back**
Angels

2 **Hello Mudduh, Hello Fadduh**
Allan Sherman

3 **If I Had a Hammer**
Trini Lopez

4 **Blue Velvet**
Bobby Vinton

5 **Candy Girl**
The Four Seasons

6 **Heat Wave**
Martha & The Vandellas

7 **Mockingbird**
Inez Foxx

8 **The Monkey Time**
Major Lance

9 **Blowin' in the Wind**
Peter, Paul and Mary

10 **Hey Girl**
Freddie Scott

UK

1 **Bad To Me**
Billy J. Kramer & The Dakotas

2 **I'm Telling You Now**
Freddie & The Dreamers

3 **She Loves You**
The Beatles

4 **It's All in the Game**
Cliff Richard

5 **I'll Never Get Over You**
Johnny Kidd & The Pirates

6 **Sweets for My Sweet**
The Searchers

7 **You Don't Have to be a Baby To Cry**
The Caravelles

8 **Wipeout**
The Surfaris

9 **Just Like Eddie**
Heinz

10 **I Want to Stay Here**
Steve Lawrence and Eydie Gorme

Bobby Vinton – red roses, blue velvet

The *Hootenanny* dispute rumbles on. A fortnight after Martin Luther Kings' speech, ABC-TV magnanimously decide that Pete Seeger can grace their programme, provided only that he signs an oath of loyalty to the United States. Seeger declines.

On the pop chart Bobby Vinton's 'Blue Velvet' succeeds the Angels' 'My Boyfriend's Back' at #1. Both are records that could have been made at any time in the last five years.

Once unthinkable, but now becoming less so, is the spectre of no American records on the British chart. On the 7th there are only four in the Top Twenty – the Surfaris' instrumental 'Wipeout' at #8, Steve Lawrence and Eydie Gorme's 'I Want to Stay Here' at #13, the Crystals' 'Da Doo Ron Ron'

at #16 and Elvis Presley's 'Devil in Disguise' at #20.

The Beatles' latest, 'She Loves You', has entered at #3, prior to a four-week run at the top. In the US it has been released, like 'Please Please Me' and 'From Me to You', on the small Swan label, following rejection by EMI's American affiliate, Capitol.

Lennon and McCartney have written the first release for fellow-Scouser and

Epstein client Cilla Black. 'Love of the Loved' only scrapes into the Top Forty, but Black will have a successful decade covering American hits, beginning with Dionne Warwick's 'Anyone Who Had a Heart' early in 1964.

The Rolling Stones are on their first British tour, supporting the Everlys, Bo Diddley and (later) Little Richard.

USA

1 **Blue Velvet**
Bobby Vinton

2 **Sally, Go 'round the Roses**
The Jaynetts

3 **Be My Baby**
The Ronettes

4 **Sugar Shack**
Jimmy Gilmer &
The Fireballs

5 **Cry Baby**
Garnet Mimms &
The Enchanters

6 **My Boyfriend's Back**
Angels

7 **Wonderful! Wonderful!**
Tymes

8 **Heat Wave**
Martha & The Vandellas

9 **Busted**
Ray Charles

10 **Then He Kissed Me**
The Crystals

Peter, Paul and Mary hold the top two positions on the album chart with their *Peter, Paul and Mary* and the new *In the Wind*, which includes several Dylan compositions. Dylan himself plays Carnegie Hall again, this time to rapturous strangers, and sales of his album *Freewheelin'* accelerate with the publicity afforded by Peter, Paul and Mary's success.

The surfing craze, at least so far as music is concerned, has been edged to one side by hot-rodding. The Beach Boys' 'Little Deuce Coupe' has reached #15; Jan and Dean are waiting in the wings with 'Drag City' and the inimitable 'Dead Man's Curve'.

Fats Domino enters the US Top Forty for the last time with 'Red Sails in the Sunset'. It's his thirty-sixth entry since 1955.

In Britain the Springfields are dissolved by lead singer Dusty Springfield's decision to go solo. Her first single, 'I Only Want to be with You', released in November, will reach #4 on the British chart and #12 on the American. The application of a white soul vocal style to essentially Middle-of-the-Road material will make her one of the few consistently successful British solo artists, on both sides of the Atlantic, over the next five years.

On the 29th '50s star Michael Holliday commits suicide. Two ghosts are in the British charts – Buddy Holly's voice with 'Wishing', and Eddie Cochran's spirit in Heinz's 'Just Like Eddie'.

In France, as if to demonstrate that Beatlemania is nothing new, 40,000 mourners attend the funeral of the 'Little Sparrow', Edith Piaf.

UK

1 **She Loves You**
The Beatles

2 **Do You Love Me?**
Brian Poole & The Tremeloes

3 **Then He Kissed Me**
The Crystals

4 **It's All in the Game**
Cliff Richard

5 **If I Had a Hammer**
Trini Lopez

6 **I Want to Stay Here**
Steve Lawrence and
Eydie Gorme

7 **Just Like Eddie**
Heinz

8 **Shindig**
The Shadows

9 **Blue Bayou/Mean Woman Blues**
Roy Orbison

10 **I'll Never Get Over You**
Johnny Kidd & The Pirates

Surf and drag kings Jan and Dean.
Inset: Fats Domino

Beatlemania is here. At the end of October, the boys have returned from Sweden to an airport full of screaming fans. On the 4th they do the Royal Command Performance. After asking most of the audience – 'you in the cheap seats' – to clap their hands, Lennon addresses the Royal Box with the suggestion that 'the rest of you just rattle your jewellery'. The Beatles are becoming more than their music – like the folk movement in the US they are becoming the focus for a wider ranger of social and generational attitudes.

Not that this will matter a jot if the music fails. It doesn't. On the 22nd the second album, *With the Beatles*, is released; on the 29th the fifth single, 'I Want to Hold Your Hand'. The creative edge seems to be growing ever sharper.

The North still rules Britain. Gerry and the Pacemakers have their third consecutive #1 with future football anthem 'You'll Never Walk Alone'. The Searchers reach #2 with their second, 'Sugar and Spice'. Manchester's Hollies and Freddie and the

USA

1 **Sugar Shack**
Jimmy Gilmer & The Fireballs
2 **Deep Purple**
Nino Tempo & April Stevens
3 **Washington Square**
Village Stompers
4 **Busted**
Ray Charles
5 **Mean Woman Blues**
Roy Orbison
6 **Donna the Prima Donna**
Dion Di Muci
7 **I Can't Stay Mad at You**
Skeeter Davis
8 **Be My Baby**
The Ronettes
9 **It's All Right**
The Impressions
10 **Maria Elena**
Los Indios Tabajaras

UK

1 **You'll Never Walk Alone**
Gerry & The Pacemakers
2 **She Loves You**
The Beatles
3 **Do You Love Me?**
Brian Poole & The Tremeloes
4 **Blue Bayou/Mean Woman Blues**
Roy Orbison
5 **Then He Kissed Me**
The Crystals
6 **If I Had a Hammer**
Trini Lopez
7 **I Who Have Nothing**
Shirley Bassey
8 **Sugar and Spice**
The Searchers
9 **Let It Rock /Memphis Tennessee**
Chuck Berry
10 **The First Time**
Adam Faith

Beatlemania

Dreamers are both in the Top Twenty. The Rolling Stones' new release, 'I Wanna be Your Man', is a Lennon-McCartney song.

The other great London groups are yet to appear. The Kinks, still the Ravens, are making a demo; the Who, still the Detours, are playing R&B sets around the capital. The Small Faces haven't yet met, though Steve Marriott has released an unsuccessful single for Decca.

Ends and beginnings. On the same day as *With the Beatles* is released, John F. Kennedy is shot dead in Dallas. The Vietnam War is already underway. From here on in the music and the politics will get harder to untangle.

The Beatles have brought back together the musical strands which flowed from the earlier fusion of pop, R&B and country. All the various elements – from Chuck Berry to mainstream pop, the Everlys to Motown – can be seen and heard in their songs, self-penned and otherwise. But they also represent something more than a bringing together. Through their genius for melody, their wit, intelligence and boundless exuberance, the Beatles have transcended their musical roots, and

campuses the folk explosion continues. California has Spector and the Beach Boys, both pioneers of the new emphasis on production over performance. New York pushes out girl group hits, Detroit harbours Motown's developing excellence, Nashville remains the capital of country music. R&B still emerges from traditional centres like Chicago, New Orleans and Memphis.

The next great cross-breeding of styles will involve the British groups and the American folk movement – in short, the Beatles and Dylan –

USA

1 **Dominique**
Singing Nun

2 **I'm Leaving It up to You**
Dale and Grace

3 **Everybody**
Tommy Roe

4 **Louie Louie**
Kingsmen

5 **She's a Fool**
Lesley Gore

6 **Sugar Shack**
Jimmy Gilmer & The Fireballs

7 **You Don't Have to Be a Baby to Cry**
The Caravelles

8 **Be True to Your School**
Beach Boys

9 **Washington Square**
Village Stompers

10 **Walking the Dog**
Rufus Thomas

UK

1 **She Loves You**
The Beatles

2 **Don't Talk to Him**
Cliff Richard

3 **You Were Made For Me**
Freddie & The Dreamers

4 **You'll Never Walk Alone**
Gerry & The Pacemakers

5 **Secret Love**
Kathy Kirby

6 **I'll Keep You Satisfied**
Billy J. Kramer & The Dakotas

7 **Maria Elena**
Los Indios Tabajaros

8 **Glad All Over**
The Dave Clark Five

9 **I Only Want to be with You**
Dusty Springfield

10 **I Want to Hold Your Hand**
The Beatles

created a new beginning for popular music.

On the 26th, after a year of rejection, Capitol launches 'I Want to Hold Your Hand' on an unsuspecting and splintered American music scene. On the college

but each of these other numerous strands will offer its own seeds to the numerous cross-fertilizations of the late '60s and early '70s.

As the year ends one crucial meeting occurs. The Searchers are recording

'Needles and Pins', a song written by Los Angeles' Sonny Bono and Jack Nitzsche. It's decided to let the softer-voiced Mike Pender and Chris Curtis harmonize above a raft of jangling guitars. Liverpool meets California.

The Searchers

Index of Artists and Bands

Numbers in italic refer to illustrations

General Index

Index of Song Titles